Pilgrimage: A Very Short Introduction

VERY SHORT INTRODUCTIONS are for anyone wanting a stimulating and accessible way into a new subject. They are written by experts, and have been translated into more than 40 different languages.

The series began in 1995, and now covers a wide variety of topics in every discipline. The VSI library now contains over 350 volumes—a Very Short Introduction to everything from Psychology and Philosophy of Science to American History and Relativity—and continues to grow in every subject area.

Very Short Introductions available now:

ACCOUNTING Christopher Nobes
ADVERTISING Winston Fletcher
AFRICAN AMERICAN RELIGION
    Eddie S. Glaude Jr.
AFRICAN HISTORY John Parker and
    Richard Rathbone
AFRICAN RELIGIONS Jacob K. Olupona
AGNOSTICISM Robin Le Poidevin
ALEXANDER THE GREAT Hugh Bowden
AMERICAN HISTORY Paul S. Boyer
AMERICAN IMMIGRATION
    David A. Gerber
AMERICAN LEGAL HISTORY
    G. Edward White
AMERICAN POLITICAL HISTORY
    Donald Critchlow
AMERICAN POLITICAL PARTIES
    AND ELECTIONS L. Sandy Maisel
AMERICAN POLITICS
    Richard M. Valelly
THE AMERICAN PRESIDENCY
    Charles O. Jones
AMERICAN SLAVERY
    Heather Andrea Williams
THE AMERICAN WEST Stephen Aron
AMERICAN WOMEN'S HISTORY
    Susan Ware
ANAESTHESIA Aidan O'Donnell
ANARCHISM Colin Ward
ANCIENT ASSYRIA Karen Radner
ANCIENT EGYPT Ian Shaw
ANCIENT EGYPTIAN ART AND
    ARCHITECTURE Christina Riggs
ANCIENT GREECE Paul Cartledge

THE ANCIENT NEAR EAST
    Amanda H. Podany
ANCIENT PHILOSOPHY Julia Annas
ANCIENT WARFARE Harry Sidebottom
ANGELS David Albert Jones
ANGLICANISM Mark Chapman
THE ANGLO-SAXON AGE John Blair
THE ANIMAL KINGDOM
    Peter Holland
ANIMAL RIGHTS David DeGrazia
THE ANTARCTIC Klaus Dodds
ANTISEMITISM Steven Beller
ANXIETY Daniel Freeman and
    Jason Freeman
THE APOCRYPHAL GOSPELS
    Paul Foster
ARCHAEOLOGY Paul Bahn
ARCHITECTURE Andrew Ballantyne
ARISTOCRACY William Doyle
ARISTOTLE Jonathan Barnes
ART HISTORY Dana Arnold
ART THEORY Cynthia Freeland
ASTROBIOLOGY David C. Catling
ATHEISM Julian Baggini
AUGUSTINE Henry Chadwick
AUSTRALIA Kenneth Morgan
AUTISM Uta Frith
THE AVANT GARDE David Cottington
THE AZTECS David Carrasco
BACTERIA Sebastian G. B. Amyes
BARTHES Jonathan Culler
THE BEATS David Sterritt
BEAUTY Roger Scruton
BESTSELLERS John Sutherland

Available soon:

For more information visit our website

www.oup.com/vsi/

Ian Reader

PILGRIMAGE

A Very Short Introduction

OXFORD
UNIVERSITY PRESS

OXFORD

UNIVERSITY PRESS

Great Clarendon Street, Oxford, OX2 6DP,
United Kingdom

Oxford University Press is a department of the University of Oxford.
It furthers the University's objective of excellence in research, scholarship,
and education by publishing worldwide. Oxford is a registered trade mark of
Oxford University Press in the UK and in certain other countries

First edition published in 2015

Impression: 4

Published in the United States of America by Oxford University Press
198 Madison Avenue, New York, NY 10016, United States of America

British Library Cataloguing in Publication Data
Data available

Library of Congress Control Number: 2014954757

ISBN 978-0-19-871822-2

Printed in Great Britain by
Ashford Colour Press Ltd, Gosport, Hampshire

Contents

Contents

List of illustrations

Chapter 1
Pilgrimage around the world

Pilgrimage is a global phenomenon found almost universally across cultures. Large numbers of pilgrimage places—from major religious institutions with national and international reputations, to regional shrines and local copies of major pilgrimages—have developed and flourished historically and in the modern day. Catholic pilgrimage centres such as the shrine of Our Lady of Guadalupe in Mexico and of Lourdes in France now attract several million visitors a year. Millions of Muslims from around the globe make pilgrimages to Islam's holy sites of Mecca and Medina in Saudi Arabia every year, including two or more million during the annual *hajj* pilgrimage period. Thousands of walkers and cyclists follow the Camino, the pilgrim's way across Europe to the cathedral at Santiago de Compostela in north-west Spain, which is said to hold the relics of St James, while many more go there each year by bus, plane, and train (see Figure 1). In Japan large numbers of pilgrims wearing white shrouds and carrying pilgrims' staffs make a 1,400-kilometre circuit of the island of Shikoku that takes them to eighty-eight Buddhist temples in the company, according to pilgrimage lore, of the mendicant Buddhist holy man Kōbō Daishi. While many do so by foot, on a journey that can take six or more weeks, the vast majority go by bus or car, often in organized tour groups led by a priest or pilgrimage guide, that take only a few days.

1. Pilgrim walking on the Camino to Santiago de Compostela.

Such pilgrimages have attracted plentiful media and public attention, and have been the focus of best-selling books, films, and television documentaries that have heightened their profile. In 2001, for instance, the German comedian Hape Kerkeling walked on pilgrimage to Santiago de Compostela, and then wrote a book about his experiences (which was later translated into English)—selling millions of copies, topping the best-seller charts in Germany, and inspiring large numbers of Germans to follow in his footsteps. Other writer-pilgrims include Shirley MacLaine and Paulo Coelho, whose 'New Age' style best-sellers have encouraged many people to do the pilgrimage. Television documentaries and films such as *The Way*, starring Martin Sheen and focusing on the experiences of an American pilgrim to Santiago, have added to its popularity. In Japan, the Shikoku pilgrimage has been the focus of several documentaries, especially by NHK (Japan's national broadcaster), that have highlighted its history, scenery, and associations with Japanese tradition. It has also featured prominently in a number of Japanese films and TV dramas in recent years, while the publication of a large number of memoirs by pilgrims has further made the pilgrimage into a media phenomenon in Japan, just as the Santiago Camino has become in Europe.

This picture of large numbers of pilgrims on the move and of heightened public and media interest in the practice is evident also in India, where millions of Hindus embark on pilgrimages to Hindu holy cities such as Hardwar and Varanasi, where pilgrims bathe in the River Ganges. In India, too, every three years the Kumbh Mela, a mass pilgrimage described as the world's largest human gathering and centred on ritual bathing, attracts millions (see Figure 2). In 1989 the estimated number who came to bathe at the Kumbh Mela at Allahabad, where the Ganges and the River Yamuna (along with a mythical river, the Saraswati) meet, was around 15 million; in 2013 that number had grown to between 80 and 100 million. The Kumbh Mela attracts massive attention in the Indian and international media, along with visits by Indian politicians for whom a ritual bath during the Mela can enhance their Hindu credentials. Many other shrines and temples around

2. Pilgrims bathing at the Kumbh Mela, Allahabad.

the country attract large pilgrim numbers, including formerly remote mountain sites that have become more accessible because of improved transport links and other facilities. Shri Mata Vaishno Devi shrine in Jammu, north-west India, for example, has benefited from the development of new lodging facilities, roads, and even a helicopter pad and services that enable wealthy pilgrims swift access to the shrine. Such developments along with skilful mass publicity by shrine authorities have raised the site's national profile and produced an exponential rise in pilgrim numbers in recent times.

In the disputed mountainous area of Kashmir thousands of Hindu pilgrims make the trek to the cave-temple of Amarnath, sacred to the deity Shiva, during the brief summer season when the mountain passes are open. This pilgrimage, which has been the focus of attacks by terrorists who dispute India's claims in the region, is nowadays heavily protected by the Indian Army. It has also been assiduously promoted by Hindu nationalists in order to advance Indian claims in the region. In 1971, I took part in the Amarnath pilgrimage; at that time there were relatively few pilgrims, facilities were rudimentary, and there was little logistical support. The situation was similar in the 1980s, with officials estimating that 12,000 people made the pilgrimage in 1989. By 2011 numbers had risen to over 630,000, thanks to nationalist campaigns that had heightened the pilgrimage's profile and to massive logistical support from the government and Army, including plentiful accommodation facilities and better transport developments that have reduced the distances pilgrims have to walk.

Religious cultures and multiple pilgrimages

The pilgrimages that have been introduced here are but a small sample of the many pilgrimage sites around the world and across religious traditions that have prominent reputations and are attracting pilgrims in the present day. Within virtually every religious tradition and geographical area one can find plentiful other examples that have over the ages attracted visitors, whether from afar or from closer at hand. Christianity (notably Catholicism) has developed extensive numbers of pilgrimage sites wherever it has spread, often associated with apparitions of the Virgin Mary. These include Knock in Ireland, where in 1879 villagers had a vision in which the Virgin Mary appeared on the side of the local chapel, and which has subsequently been described as Ireland's national pilgrimage site; and Medjugorje in Herzegovina, to which many Catholics flocked after Marian apparitions were seen by a group of young people in the 1980s.

Catholicism's spread to Latin America was accompanied by the appearance of Catholic pilgrimage sites there, including the aforementioned Guadalupe, while African Christian cultures, similarly, have developed networks of sites to which the faithful travel. Ethiopia's long Christian history, for example, incorporates several significant pilgrimage sites, such as Axum, where the Cathedral of St Mary of Zion is said to house the Ark of the Covenant, and Lalibela, whose rock-hewn churches were built eight centuries ago by King Lalibela in order to create a 'new Jerusalem' in his realm by symbolically reproducing that city's structure, and which are a continuing magnet for Ethiopian Christians and, nowadays, for tourists worldwide.

Buddhists from around the world travel to Bodh Gaya, the site of the Buddha's enlightenment in India, and to other sites associated with his life's journey, while numerous Buddhist temples serve as pilgrimage destinations for their national and local communities. For Burmese Buddhists the Shwedagon Temple, in the capital Yangon, is a major national pilgrimage site housing hair relics said to be from the Buddha. The Temple of the Tooth in Kandy, Sri Lanka, which has a Buddha tooth relic, is a magnet for Sri Lankan Buddhist devotees. Shikoku is nowadays Japan's most popular Buddhist pilgrimage, while Japan's other main

5

religious tradition, Shinto, has many pilgrimage sites, including the Great Shrines of Ise, which have close links to Japan's foundation myths and its Imperial family.

While Mecca and Medina may be the best-known pilgrimage sites in Islam, many others play significant roles in the devotional lives of Muslims, internationally, nationally, and regionally. In Mashhad, Iran, the shrine of Imam Reza commemorating the 9th century martyrdom of the eighth Imam of the Shi'ite Muslim tradition is a major focus of devotional travel for Shi'ites in general and Iranians in particular, while the 12th century Sufi saint Moinuddin Chishti's shrine in Ajmer, India, attracts millions of Indian Muslims each year (as well as many from other faiths). In India, too, the Sikh tradition has its network of pilgrimage places, including the Golden Temple in Amritsar, Sikhism's holiest site and main pilgrimage centre.

As new religious traditions develop, they frequently create their own special pilgrimage centres. The Japanese new religion, Tenrikyō, developed in the 19th century by its visionary founder, Nakayama Miki, regards Tenri, where Nakayama lived and received her revelations, as the sacred centre of humanity, to which all should return to worship. Pilgrimage there is a core activity of Tenrikyō devotees, especially on 26 January each year, the anniversary of Nakayama's passing. The International Society for Krishna Consciousness (ISKCON), better known as the Hare Krishna movement, was founded in 1966 by an Indian guru and has grown primarily in Western countries, developing its own pilgrimage centres for the faithful. For example, Bhaktivedanta Manor in Hertfordshire, close to London, is the movement's British centre and a major site of pilgrimage for Hare Krishna devotees, as well as for Hindus resident in the United Kingdom.

Not all pilgrimage sites are specific to one faith. Jerusalem has great significance in Judaism, Christianity, and Islam, and is a site of pilgrimage for all three (see Figure 3); in Sri Lanka, Sri Pada is a

3. Contested places: the Western Wall and the Dome of the Rock, Jerusalem.

mountain pilgrimage site visited by Buddhists, Christian, Hindus, and Muslims; and Kataragama, in the jungle of southern Sri Lanka, is especially important to the island's Hindus and Buddhists. While this can produce mutual feelings of harmony as different faiths share common ground, it can often produce tensions and conflicts grounded both in differences of faith and because of competing ethnic, religious, and political claims—an issue clearly evident in Jerusalem in modern times. At Kataragama, tensions reflecting the recent conflict between the primarily Hindu Tamils and the Singhalese Buddhists have surfaced, as have strains over the expansion of Singhalese Buddhist influences in what was once a primarily Hindu site.

Localization, proliferation, and replication

Not all pilgrimage places are internationally significant or widely known; many are essentially local in nature. I have two Japanese pilgrimage encyclopaedias on my desk, each listing several hundred in the country, and I have visited several dozen pilgrimage routes when living and travelling in Japan. Only a few are nationally prominent, and most cater just for local clienteles. Such local pilgrimages are significant in the wider world of pilgrimage, for they have long provided a means through which people unable to travel far can perform pilgrimages and seek their benefits. Most people in medieval England, for example, would have found it difficult to get away from their homes for any length of time or to have the wherewithal to walk to prominent but distant pilgrimage shrines such as Canterbury. They did, however, have numerous local shrines and holy wells to which they could make short visits to pray for various blessings.

The same holds true for countries such as India where, besides nationally significant sites such as Varanasi and major gatherings such as the Kumbh Mela, many thousands of local and regional pilgrimage sites are visited by local clienteles, either to seek here-and-now benefits or because they are unable to travel farther afield. In her study of pilgrimage practices in India, for example, the American scholar Ann Gold talks about how Rajasthani villagers make occasional long-distance pilgrimages on special occasions, such as to perform death rituals for close relatives, while making more frequent short pilgrimages to local shrines to pray for more immediate needs.

Sometimes local pilgrimages involve replications of more famed and distant ones. Small-scale replicas of prominent temples such as Varanasi's Sri Vishwanath are found widely in India, often in the courtyards of other temples, to enable people who are far from Varanasi, for example, to nonetheless 'visit' it. Many pilgrimages in Japan are copies in regional or miniature versions of major pilgrimages, such as Shikoku, often, in this case, with eighty-eight stone statues or wayside shrines representing Shikoku's eighty-eight temples. Many islands in Japan's Inland Sea have their own smaller-scale versions of the Shikoku pilgrimage, often with local miracle stories and tales of Kōbō Daishi apparitions. While the Shikoku pilgrimage may take six weeks or so to walk, such smaller-scale island pilgrimages would usually take just a few days. Walking the Shikoku pilgrimage took my wife and I forty days in 1984: doing the eighty-eight-stage Shikoku replica pilgrimage around the Inland Sea island of Shōdoshima took us just one week the following year. Other Shikoku replicas may consist of just a set of eighty-eight stones under each of which soil from one of the Shikoku temples has been placed; such pilgrimages, which enable people to 'walk' the route in a few minutes, are known as *sunafumi* 'stepping on the soil (of Shikoku)' pilgrimages.

At Kaiganji, a temple in Shikoku, there is one such small-scale version that replicates in microcosm the physical structure of the Shikoku pilgrimage. In a route one-kilometre long, one visits all eighty-eight temples—which are spaced out in proportion to how they are placed on the actual route—one walks on their soil, and one passes statues and tableaux depicting popular stories from pilgrimage legends. One tableau depicts Kōbō Daishi with a rich miser, Emon Saburō, who had insulted the holy man and refused him alms. Emon, as a result, was cursed and had to go on the pilgrimage to seek forgiveness; as Emon lay dying, Kōbō Daishi appeared before him to absolve him of his sins (see Figure 4). This legend underpins beliefs that doing the pilgrimage will eradicate bad karma and lead to salvation. Performing such miniaturized versions not only stands in for the main pilgrimage for those unable to do the longer journey, but also, as priests at Kaiganji told me, it enables those who had done the Shikoku pilgrimage previously to remember and reawaken their experiences there—perhaps even inspiring them to do it again.

Themes of replication are also found in Christian contexts. In 1061 a widowed Anglo-Saxon noblewoman saw an apparition of the Virgin Mary at Walsingham in Norfolk, England, in which Mary asked her to build a replica there of Jesus's family house at Nazareth. This transplantation thus enabled people to 'visit' a distant holy Christian site within their own locality. Walsingham became the centre of a Marian cult that developed into one of the most

4. Kōbō Daishi forgiving the rich miser Emon Saburō, at Kaiganji's replica pilgrimage site, Shikoku.

prominent English pilgrimage sites until it was suppressed during the Reformation. It was revived in the late 19th century and, in the guise of Our Lady of Walsingham, has become a major English pilgrimage site for Catholics and Anglicans.

King Lalibela's rock churches in Ethiopia constructed to symbolize Jerusalem are another example of this localized reproduction of the universality of major pilgrimage sites. Lourdes is another site that has been replicated worldwide, allowing people unable to go physically to Lourdes to share in its reputed spiritual and healing benefits. During the 19th century, Lourdes replica grottoes developed in the USA for the benefit of American Catholics unable to travel to Europe, and they can still be found in places as diverse as the Bronx in New York and the campus of Notre Dame University in Indiana. There are several Lourdes grottoes in Japan as well as in the UK. I have 'been' to Lourdes in both countries, at Cleator Moor in Cumbria, which is the focus of an annual pilgrimage from the

Catholic diocese of Lancaster, and in Tokyo, where a Lourdes grotto stands in the grounds of the Catholic cathedral.

Diaspora communities also may take their pilgrimage traditions with them. The Japanese who emigrated to Hawaii in the late 19th century to work in the sugar plantations, for example, constructed small-scale Shikoku replicas there, while Hindu communities in the UK and USA have built their own versions of prominent Indian pilgrimage sites in their new countries of residence. In such terms, pilgrimage sites can be transferable and infinitely reproducible in ways that bring their universality to people far distant from the 'real' physical site. This transferability is now even emerging online in the guise of virtual pilgrimages through which people can 'visit' pilgrimage sites on the internet.

History, popularity, and change

The popularity of pilgrimage is not just a modern phenomenon. Many of the pilgrimages that have been mentioned have long histories of attracting pilgrims. Santiago de Compostela was one of the most important sites of medieval Christianity and received pilgrims from all over Europe, while in 18th and 19th century Japan pilgrims to the Ise shrines in some years numbered in the millions. This does not mean that the same pilgrimages have flourished across the ages or that popular pilgrimage sites will always remain so. Canterbury Cathedral, with its shrine to St Thomas Becket, was a major magnet for pilgrims in the era after Becket's murder there in 1170. However, competition, notably from Marian shrines such as Walsingham, meant that by the 16th century Canterbury's income from pilgrims was less than a twentieth of what it had been in the 13th.

When, in mid-19th century France, reports circulated of an apparition of the Virgin Mary at Lourdes, followed by stories of miraculous healing, this led to the development of one of the most popular pilgrimage sites in the Catholic world. However, while Lourdes' emergence certainly increased pilgrimage activities in France, it also drew pilgrims away from other French Marian shrines. The Santiago Camino certainly attracts large numbers of pilgrims nowadays, just as it had previously flourished in the medieval period. In between, however, things were rather different, with pilgrim numbers falling until, by the mid-19th century, it had become virtually moribund before strenuous efforts by church and other authorities helped revive it. Similarly, the Shikoku pilgrimage has fluctuated in popularity over the centuries; I have interviewed pilgrims, priests, and local residents who remembered Shikoku in the late 1940s and who told me that the temples were rundown with virtually no pilgrims. It was not until organized pilgrimage bus tours started to develop in the early 1950s that the pilgrimage underwent a revival leading to the crowds mentioned earlier.

Pilgrimages not only wax and wane in popularity; they also die out. A recent study in the Netherlands identified over 600 pilgrimage sites within this relatively small country—testimony to the ubiquity of pilgrimage—and showed that some 250 were still extant. The others appeared, in effect, to be defunct. Local research there on the Japanese Inland Sea island of Awaji shows that at different eras various pilgrimage routes have flourished there, but that in so doing they have often displaced other pilgrimages in terms of popularity and caused them to fall into disuse. When new pilgrimages arise or as particular sites experience rapid growth, they may increase the general number of pilgrims around the world. They may also, however, draw people away from other sites and cause their decline and even demise, for the world of pilgrimage is an arena of fluctuating fortunes, in which large numbers of pilgrims at one site in one era need not mean continued success across the board.

'Secular' and 'nonreligious' pilgrimages

An example of how the culture of pilgrimage may adapt to, or be manifest in contemporary settings, is the growth of what are described as either 'secular' or 'nonreligious' pilgrimages: places that have no official religious affiliation but whose visitors may refer to themselves as pilgrims and who perform actions that resonate with what goes on at places such as Lourdes, Santiago, and Shikoku. Public memorials associated with death and grief, such as the Vietnam Memorial Wall in Washington, DC, for example, can fall into this category. Places linked to the worlds of popular culture, especially when linked to celebrity deaths and memorials, may be viewed as sites imbued with special meanings by fans and devotees. Graceland, Elvis Presley's house in Memphis, USA, is one such place, visited annually by millions, many of whom leave offerings and messages to the 'King' at Graceland's gates and at his grave while viewing their visits there as pilgrimages.

These places and the phenomena surrounding them will be looked at in Chapter 6, along with another aspect of contemporary development: how existing sites may be adopted by newly emergent traditions. These include places such as Glastonbury, in England, and Sedona in the USA—the former historically a Christian pilgrimage site and the latter important in Native American religious culture—both of which have more recently become centres for New Age devotees, who make pilgrimages there while claiming to eschew any formal religious affiliations.

The pilgrimage industry and tourism

Pilgrimage is also a major industry, promoted not just by religious authorities to increase faith, but also by commercial concerns such as tourist agencies and transport firms. Such commercial involvement and the infrastructures it provides—from good transport and accommodation facilities to information provided by guidebooks and, nowadays, online services that help pilgrims plan their journeys—are important factors in the growth of pilgrimage.

Sometimes labelled as 'spiritual tourism', 'religious tourism', or 'pilgrimage tourism', pilgrimage generates vast sums of money every year; keeps many hundreds of thousands employed; and is a major source of income for the people living in the vicinity of major sites. The economy of Lourdes centres almost wholly around its pilgrimage, while a saying in Mecca—that people there do not need agriculture because they benefit from an annual 'crop' of pilgrims—further indicates the economic importance of pilgrimage. In Shikoku, the pilgrimage, thanks to the industry—from local bus firms to restaurants, lodges, and souvenir shops—that has grown around it, is an increasingly important element in the island's economy. In such terms it is unsurprising that various agencies and interest groups, such as tourist offices, regional governments, commercial firms, and transport companies, have an interest in pilgrimage and may play active roles in promoting it.

This has led to concerns about the apparent commercialization of pilgrimage and its transformation from a seemingly 'spiritual' activity into one centred around markets and tourism. One should not, however, think that such developments or commercializations are simply products of the modern day any more than one should think that pilgrims were necessarily only interested in spiritual issues in earlier eras. Complaints about corruption and commercialism, the clusters of souvenir shops around shrines, and the behaviour of visitors, who appear to be little more than tourists, reverberate across history. In medieval times, Christian pilgrims and priests alike grumbled about exploitation and mercenary behaviour by the merchants who transported them to the Christian Holy Land, while religious authorities often spoke disdainfully about the unruly behaviour of pilgrims. Pilgrims to Ise in 18th and 19th century Japan were well known for their readiness to make use of the town's many bars, brothels, and souvenir shops; indeed, a satirical poem of the era even suggested that it was these activities, rather than worshipping at the shrines, that primarily motivated pilgrims.

From its early days the attractions of Lourdes included not just its grotto and healing stories, but the shops, entertainment facilities, and modern sights that grew in the town. From the outset, too, complaints were levelled at the commercialism and cheap souvenirs of Lourdes. Contemporary criticisms reiterate much of what has been said about pilgrimage in the past, but the reality is that commerce, entertainment, tourist behaviour, and the ready engagement with them of pilgrims have been elements in the structure of pilgrimage over the ages. They have, indeed, been means through which shrines have been able to sustain themselves economically and through which those who help lodge and support pilgrims are able to make a living. They often also provide pilgrims with diversions that help them deal with the intense emotions of pilgrimages as well as motivating them to travel in the first place.

Pilgrimage and the roots of tourism

In earlier eras, indeed, pilgrimage was often the only means whereby people could travel at all. In feudal societies, such as those of medieval Europe or Japan, mobility was greatly restricted and the idea of travel for its own sake, going on holiday, and simply getting away temporarily from one's home environment were not in themselves socially recognized activities. Pilgrimage often was the only legitimate reason that could be given for travelling; people, in order to see new places and escape from the restrictions of their local environment, in effect had to become pilgrims. The Japanese government regime from the 17th to 19th centuries restricted travel severely, but, fearful of offending the gods, they allowed people to travel when it was for religious purposes. That in turn encouraged would-be travellers to portray themselves as pilgrims. As such, while pilgrimage may have had a strong devotional element, it also clearly contained tourist elements from early on. It also developed support structures not just to help pilgrims in their enterprise but to enable people along the way and at the places to which pilgrims flocked to benefit materially from the practice.

The origins of the tourist trade are closely associated with pilgrimage, for it is generally considered that the earliest package tours were developed in the medieval era, when overland pilgrimage routes to the Christian Holy Land had become fraught with danger. By the late 13th century few made such overland journeys. They did, however, have alternative means of getting there—Venetian merchants, who controlled the Mediterranean sea-lanes and had good commercial relations with Middle Eastern authorities, offered all-inclusive, return-trip tours from their city-state to the Holy Land, with guided tours around the sites and sometimes with sightseeing stops in Egypt as well. During the 14th and 15th centuries the Holy Land pilgrimage trade was so beneficial to the Venetian economy that city authorities established a tourist office to aid pilgrims and head off their not-infrequent complaints that might damage the city's reputation and put off future pilgrims.

Elsewhere, similar services developed to enable pilgrims to travel safely to, be looked after at, and brought home from, places they had no knowledge of. In Japan, pilgrimage package tours can be found from the medieval period, while by the 17th century a flourishing tourist-style industry had developed around prominent centres such as Ise, whose guides travelled around the country recruiting pilgrims, bringing them to the shrines, and providing them with lodgings and access to shrine rituals. Such services were the precursor of modern tourist package tours, a point evident also in the role of the *sendatsu* or pilgrimage guide. The term means 'someone who stands/goes in front of' and hence guides a pilgrimage group, a role continued to this day both in Japanese pilgrimage contexts and in the spectacle of Japanese tour parties led by guides carrying flags.

To ensure safe travel, to put pilgrims' minds at rest, and to provide them with their needs such as lodgings and food when travelling or spending time at sites, an infrastructure of services has developed around most pilgrimage centres. This has contributed to the popularity of pilgrimage sites, by publicizing them and making them more readily accessible to greater numbers of people than ever before. In such ways, tourist infrastructures, transport advances, modern comforts, and advanced information systems have been important elements in the modern development and nature of pilgrimage. They have made pilgrimage more accessible to greater numbers of people, and especially to segments of society that were far less well represented in the pilgrimage world in earlier ages. The vast majority of Shikoku pilgrims prior to the 20th century, for example, were young and male; very few were elderly or female, for the lengthy route required several weeks of walking in difficult terrain with few facilities, and was difficult for all but the hardiest or for the most desperate. Nowadays, the advent of bus tours and better facilities has made pilgrimage accessible to a far wider number of people, and now not only do women outnumber men, but those over sixty form the largest single group of pilgrims. Similar pictures are found elsewhere around the world, as modern developments have democratized pilgrimage by opening it up to ever-greater numbers of people.

Familiar patterns, common grounds

Pilgrimage practices may differ across religious traditions and countries, and be enacted by people speaking different languages, expressing different faith perspectives, and even at times appearing to be less interested in formal religious orientations than in devotion to a deceased rock star, yet, at the same time, there is a readily discernible coherence and commonality across traditions. While I have mainly studied Japanese Buddhist pilgrimages, I have felt on remarkably familiar ground when visiting pilgrimage sites of other traditions elsewhere. When I look at pilgrims in Japan, I note their similarities to others elsewhere—whether in donning particular clothing to mark them out as pilgrims, as do Muslims during the *hajj* or pilgrims who, on the Santiago Camino, wear the scallop shell sign of St James, or in the acts of prayer they perform or the benefits they might seek from their pilgrimages. What goes on at and around pilgrimage shrines—often a mass of noise, people, stalls, and the buying of souvenirs, statuettes, candles, and religious charms—and the activities of those involved in the pilgrimage process appear to differ little overall from one tradition or context to another. While this does not mean that one site is the same as every other or that every pilgrim behaves similarly and has similar experiences, it does suggest that there is enough common ground across the spectrum for us to talk of pilgrimage in universal terms, as a common human phenomenon spanning cultures, religions, and continents.

The American scholar James G. Lochtefeld, who had long studied the Indian pilgrimage site of Hardwar, commented that, when he first visited the Italian pilgrimage site of Assisi, it felt familiar although he had never been there before. Hardwar and Assisi may have had their own special characteristics, but as pilgrimage sites they had enough in common to make him feel a sense of familiarity when visiting Assisi. This feeling was also emphasized by a Japanese couple I once interviewed. After having performed many pilgrimages in Japan, some (including Shikoku) many dozens of times, they branched out by visiting Buddhist pilgrimage sites in China and then went on a pilgrimage to Buddhist sites in India. Thereafter they went to European Christian sites such as Lourdes and Assisi, viewing their visits there as pilgrimages because, they told me, while they were not Christians, they were *pilgrims*. Even though they knew nothing of the languages or the cultures they were visiting, they had not felt out of place; they were in the familiar and recognizable world of pilgrimage.

A global phenomenon

Pilgrimage, then, is a global phenomenon that nowadays is attracting large numbers of people who manifest many feelings and attitudes in common. To investigate the phenomenon further, we need now to discuss what the terms 'pilgrimage' and 'pilgrim' mean, and to look more closely at some of the meanings, dynamics, and thematic elements of pilgrimage, as well as the actions of pilgrims and what motivates them, while further investigating the other themes, such as the service industry, tourism, and new forms of pilgrimage, that have been raised here.

Chapter 2
Forms, themes, and meanings

The English words 'pilgrimage' derives, via the French *pèlerinage*, from the Latin terms *peregrinus*, 'foreign', and *per ager*, 'going through the fields'. Thus it indicates the idea of journeys, travelling, leaving the comforts of home, and being a stranger in the lands through which one journeys. It was also often associated with the notion of the human being as *homo viator*—a figure on a path or journey seeking the meaning of life (and, in Christian terms, finding God). Pilgrimage as a practice certainly predates Christianity, with evidence of travel in earlier periods to sacred sites in numerous parts of the world, from ancient Greece to India to China. As a word, however, its initial origins are with Christianity, and associated with early Christian travel to places associated with significant figures (from Jesus to the multitude of saints) and key events and stories in the tradition.

Thus pilgrimage as a concept and practice incorporated themes of people leaving home, going to and performing acts of veneration at places where holy figures from their tradition had been, where significant events associated with them had occurred, and where their spiritual presence could, it was believed, still be felt. From early on, too, it contained a sense of performing spiritual exercises to bring the pilgrim closer to the divine. This did not, however, mean that pilgrims saw their journeys solely or even primarily through such a lens. Many, perhaps the vast majority, viewed their pilgrimages as a means through which to gain graces and merits that would benefit them both in life and, through the eradication of sins, after death, while praying for all manner of worldly benefits, particularly miraculous cures from maladies. They were also inspired by the idea that being in places that were marked out as specially sacred because of their links to saints and other holy figures, enabled them to directly encounter those figures and receive their grace. Other themes that accrued to the idea of pilgrimage included that of penance; by the 6th century CE, Christian ecclesiastical and other courts began to sentence wrongdoers to perform penitential pilgrimages in order to expiate their sins.

'Pilgrimage' beyond the English language

While the word 'pilgrimage' may be English, and its etymology associated with Christianity, the ideas and themes it relates to extend far beyond that language and tradition. Indeed in English this one term contains a multiplicity of nuances that may, in other languages and cultural contexts, be covered by a variety of terms indicating different forms of religiously oriented travel. In her study of pilgrimages in modern Greece, for instance, Jill Dubisch points out that Greek has a number of terms with different nuanced meanings associated with travel and worship that end up being translated in English (in effect for want of something better) by 'pilgrimage'.

It is the same for Japanese, where more than a dozen terms exist relating to travelling, praying, and worshiping at shrines and temples. All have slightly different meanings but are most conveniently translated as 'pilgrimage'. The themes evident within the Christian origins of the term, from its performance as a penance to eradicate transgressions, to concepts of searching for ultimate meaning, are also implicit in Japanese terms. *Junrei*, for example, is commonly used for one of the most prevalent forms of pilgrimage in Japan, visiting circuits of Buddhist temples, and it combines the notion of 'going around' (*jun*) and worshipping (*rei*). The origins of many Japanese Buddhist pilgrimages contain ideas of a journey on a spiritual path towards enlightenment—a symbolic theme found in the Shikoku pilgrimage—and of eradicating bad karma, through which pilgrims believe that they can ensure a better rebirth or progress to the Buddhist Pure Land at death.

The term *junrei* also indicates that pilgrimage need not be focused on a single sacred goal or site, but can include several places linked together in a wider sacred geography that encompasses a region or area. This is a prevalent mode of pilgrimage in Japan. It is also found in places such as India, where Hindu multiple site pilgrimages include the *Char Dham*, comprising four sacred places (Puri, Rameswaram, Dwarka, and Badrinath) at the four geographic corners of India; and the *saptapuri*, seven sacred cities (Ayodhya, Hardwar, Kanchipuram, Ujjain, Varanasi, Mathura, and Dwarka), famed as crossing places where deities are believed to have descended to earth and that form a linked pilgrimage circuit.

Pilgrimage is also the English term commonly used to translate *tirthayatra*, initially from Sanskrit and widely used in Hindu contexts. It incorporates the ideas of crossing (*tirtha*) and movement, travel, and procession (*yatra*). Crossing here has both physical and spiritual dimensions; *tirtha* are river crossing points and they are also, symbolically, crossing places between this and other realms, notably those of death and liberation. Many Hindu pilgrimages commemorate the dead, whose cremated ashes are carried by relatives on pilgrimage to sacred river sites, where they are placed in the water, from whence they flow to the sea, thereby allowing the departed to attain liberation and to cross to another realm. The term also refers to places where the human and divine worlds intersect, where the gods appear and may be encountered in this world. Hence pilgrimage places are seen as being especially good for encountering and beseeching the gods for favours and are places of specially charged spiritual significance, offering the possibility of liberation and worldly benefits at one and the same time.

Journeys, goals, and tensions

Pilgrimage and related terms such as *junrei* and *tirthyatra* thus contain notions of crossing, sacred geographies, movement between states of being, the integral nature of travel and worship, and of journeys to get to and be in places that are considered holy. They further indicate that pilgrimage involves both the places themselves and the practices engaged in on the way to and at them. They also point to a tension that often exists in pilgrimage between movement and place, and about whether the essence of pilgrimage is located in travel to a sacred place or primarily in the actions engaged in when there. The accounts of those who walk to Santiago de Compostela, for example, tend to emphasize the journey as the essence of pilgrimage; some pilgrims even express a sense of anticlimax at reaching their ostensible goal, the cathedral, after having become so immersed in the long path to reach it. Those who travel by plane or train direct to Santiago, may, conversely, pay less attention to the journey there than to the rituals and prayers they engage in when at the site, and may see being in the sacred place as the essence of their pilgrimage.

Ann Gold's account of her travels with Rajasthani pilgrims indicates that they viewed the religious centres where they stopped to perform their rituals as the most important aspect of their pilgrimage. Similarly, one of the most striking findings of my research on the Shikoku pilgrimage was that those who walk the route commonly view the pilgrimage path as the core of their pilgrimages and focus less on the temples themselves, which are often viewed more as reference points on, or even distractions from, the path. By contrast, those who travel by bus or car emphasize the temples as the focal point of their pilgrimages, and spend far longer, and engage in more complex acts of worship, at the temples than those who walk.

In essence, both journey and place can be key elements in pilgrimage. However, different pilgrims, depending on how they do their pilgrimages, may emphasize different aspects of it. Frequently the process of getting there may not be considered important compared to that of performing rituals and practices within the ambit of the sacred location itself. This is the case at places such as Lourdes, Mecca, and Hardwar, for example, where the large majority of pilgrims use trains, planes, and other mechanized means to get there, and where the chief focus is on the rituals performed at the sites themselves.

Wandering, restlessness, and symbolic life and death journeys

The themes of itinerancy, 'going through the fields', and being in foreign lands relate also to basic human conditions of being restless and wishing to seek new horizons and see new places. They express feelings that impel many travellers and pilgrims: that one's everyday circumstances, routines, and social contexts are restrictive, that one needs to escape from them in order to find new meanings and change one's life, that the truth is 'out there' somewhere, and that one needs to break away from one's normal life in order to find it. Pilgrimage has long provided a prime mechanism through which people have striven to deal with such feelings. Indeed, in many religious contexts it has been interpreted symbolically as an externalized enactment of a spiritual journey through life, perhaps as a journey to God or to enlightenment.

It may also in such terms be equated symbolically with the life stories of religious founders, which provide inspirational motifs for those who follow them. Walking in their footsteps is often a key element in pilgrimage. In Buddhism, for instance, pilgrimage may be emphasized as a means of expressing, temporarily, the themes of renunciation and detachment from the delusions of this world. Such notions were enacted by the Buddha when he left home and spent years wandering through northern India seeking enlightenment. His life journey is thus seen as a form of pilgrimage, while the key sites involved with it form one of the earliest Buddhist pilgrimage routes in India. This replicates the Buddha's life journey by visiting four key sites associated with it: Lumbini, where he was born (and from whence he fled his palatial home); Bodh Gaya, where he became enlightened; Sarnath, where he preached his first sermon, thereby 'turning the wheel of Law' to inaugurate Buddhism as a system of teaching; and Kushinagar, where he died.

Being a pilgrim also offers people the opportunity to temporarily cast off their normal mundane status and become akin not just to the sacred figures, in whose footsteps they walk, but also to religious specialists. This is certainly a theme of Buddhist pilgrimage. By leaving home, donning special pilgrimage clothing and entering a state of transience lay people in effect become temporarily like monks or nuns, and symbolically indicate that they are unattached to the everyday world for the duration of their pilgrimages.

They may also—reflecting a theme that is widespread in pilgrimage across cultures—indicate that they are temporarily dead to the everyday world. The pilgrimage clothing worn by Japanese pilgrims in Shikoku, for example, is redolent with the symbolism of death. Pilgrims there traditionally wear a white pilgrimage shroud that signifies purity and death; a bamboo hat that symbolizes the pilgrim's coffin and is inscribed with a poem signifying the transience of life; and a staff that symbolizes the pilgrim's gravestone and bears a mortuary inscription (see Figure 5). In such terms they are 'dead to the world' while on pilgrimage. Indeed, it is not uncommon for those who have done the pilgrimage to be placed in their coffin at death dressed as pilgrims, to indicate that they are embarking on a final journey to the next realm.

Such death symbolism is also suffused with images of rebirth and renewal, in which the pilgrim, on completing the pilgrimage, is

5. Shikoku pilgrims wearing traditional clothing marked with an invocation to Kōbō Daishi.

spiritually reborn and returns, reinvigorated, to the mundane world. These themes of the pilgrimage as journey to higher spiritual states, as a life journey, an encounter with the world beyond this, and a means of renewal and reinvigoration in this world, are not limited to Buddhist pilgrimage but are widely found across pilgrimage cultures. Thus the Christian pilgrimage to Jerusalem has traditionally been seen not merely as a physical journey to a distant land but as a spiritual journey to another realm, while Hindu pilgrimages to sacred crossing places may be full of images and symbolic themes of transition from one realm to another, and of renewal and reinvigoration for those who return to their homes afterwards.

Goals, geography, and the extraordinary

While pilgrimage reflects the human condition of restlessness, it is not aimless; there is somewhere specific to go, a goal and destination, often (as with the Santiago Camino or the Shikoku pilgrimage) a route to follow along with ritual actions to be performed. While in the abstract the goal may be associated with spiritual union or enlightenment, in practical terms it invariably means going to and being at specific places that have particular resonance for the pilgrim and his/her faith, where, it is believed, spiritual forces and deities can be encountered and venerated, where their powers and the worldly benefits that flow from them can be assimilated, and/or where pilgrims can stand in the place where their spiritual leaders stood.

Pilgrimages thus are associated with human perceptions of the extraordinary and with specific locales and buildings that are believed to contain powers that transcend the everyday nature of the world. Sometimes (and notably in much of Asia) this perception of the extraordinary is manifest in geographical features. Striking geographical landscapes can, in and of themselves, be a crucial element in the formation of a pilgrimage site, especially when they are associated with life-giving forces such as water. Rivers, as has been noted, are particularly important in Hindu contexts, not simply because of their symbolism as crossing places, but also because of their life-giving power. Rivers such as the Ganges and Yamuna that irrigate the northern Indian plains are thus venerated (often in the form of deities) for this reason, while places associated with significant transitions in a river's flow, such as Gangotri, where the Ganges rises in the Himalayas, and Hardwar, where it comes down into the plains, are marked out as pilgrimage sites for such reasons.

Mountains, venerated in many cultures as holy, are frequently the focus of pilgrimages. Croagh Patrick in Ireland, which is believed to have attracted pilgrims in the pre-Christian era, became revered in Irish Catholicism as the site where Ireland's patron saint, St Patrick, reputedly fasted for forty days in the 5th century CE. Every year multitudes climb the peak in a pilgrimage on the last Sunday of July in his honour. In South Africa devotees of the Nazareth Baptist Church (also known as the Shembe Church), regard Nhlangakazi as a sacred mountain because it was there that the church's charismatic founder Isaac Shembe (1865–1935) is said to have received the spiritual revelations that led to his establishing the church. Shembe initiated pilgrimages there as a key practice in his church and each year devotees ascend the mountain, often barefoot, on a pilgrimage in which they spend several days there in prayer (see Figure 6).

Such themes of physical ascent symbolizing spiritual elevation are widely prevalent in Asia. In Hindu and Buddhist cultures

6. Shembe devotees ascending Nhlangakazi on pilgrimage.

mountains are widely viewed as the abode of gods and places where earth and higher realms meet. Many mountains in the Himalayan range are venerated in such ways because of their grandeur, while places beneath the peaks such as Gangotri are seen as locales where earthly and higher realms intersect, thus marking them out as places of pilgrimage.

Hindu and Buddhist cosmologies place a mythical mountain, Mount Meru, at the physical and spiritual centre of the world. Mount Kailas, in western Tibet, is venerated by many in these traditions as the embodiment of this mythical mountain; for Hindus, too, it is an abode of Shiva. Pilgrimage to Kailas involves not ascent but circumambulation of the mountain—thereby symbolically embracing the entire universe at whose centre Kailas is located—and is viewed by pilgrims as a journey to enlightenment. Because of its remoteness and harsh environment (plus controls on travel in the region by the ruling Chinese authorities) Kailas gets rather few pilgrims. It remains significant, however, as an example of the mountain as pilgrimage centre in the cosmological systems of the two great religious traditions that venerate it. Another is Tsari, often called Pure Crystal Mountain in English, which is seen in Tibetan Buddhism as a place where heaven and earth interpenetrate, and which is the focus of various pilgrimage devotions and practices.

In Japan, too, mountains have long been the focus of pilgrimage cults. Mounts Fuji and Ontake are (as is the case with many mountains associated with Buddhist traditions) divided symbolically into ten stages, with shrines for pilgrims to worship at each stage. The ten stages symbolically represent the ten Buddhist realms of existence, with the summit representing the final one of supreme enlightenment. Thus the mountain serves as a physical map of enlightenment, while the pilgrimage involves both a physical and a symbolic spiritual ascent. In Japan, too, a religious tradition, Shugendō, that incorporates themes from

Buddhism, Shinto, and folk religions, has developed around mountain worship and communal pilgrimage ascents of sacred mountains.

This concept of the physical landscape symbolically representing a spiritual journey or place is also evident in the development of several pilgrimage sites throughout the East Asian Buddhist world that signify the presence of Buddhist Pure Lands within this physical realm. The Pure Land of Avalokitesvara, the Buddhist figure of compassion known as Kannon in Japanese and Kuan-yin in Chinese, is conceived of as a mythical mountainous island realm of spiritual salvation where Avalokitesvara/Kuan-yin abides. Various places have been identified or designated by Buddhist monks as this-worldly representations of this Pure Land. For example, P'u-t'o-shan, a strategically well-placed island off the eastern Chinese coast at a crossroads of sea traffic, was proclaimed by monks to be Kuan-yin's spiritual realm on earth. It became the focus of major pilgrimage activities in pre-modern China, while numerous temples were built on the island to further enhance its status as a prominent Kuan-yin pilgrimage centre. In Japan, the mountainous Kumano region south of the historic capitals of Nara and Kyoto was similarly identified by monks as the physical gateway to Kannon's Pure Land and became a major focus of pilgrimage in early Japanese Buddhism.

Sacred figures, footsteps, and roots

Places associated with the origins of a faith and the figures at their core commonly become places of pilgrimage. Pilgrims to the Christian Holy Land are going to the roots of their faith, to be where Jesus walked and to follow in his footsteps. Muslims making pilgrimages to Mecca and Medina are returning to where their faith had its origins, and where the prophets of their tradition (from Ibrahim to Mohammed) engaged in the rituals and practices that are central to that faith. Ibrahim (Abraham in the Judaeo-Christian context) is viewed in Islam as the first to renounce idols and to call for veneration of one true creator god. According to Islamic tradition, he built the first temple to this one god, centred on the Ka'aba, the structure that stands in the middle of the main mosque in Mecca, and that houses the black rock that Islamic tradition says was sent to him by Allah.

In 632 CE, the final year of his life, Mohammed, Islam's final prophet, made his 'farewell pilgrimage' to his home city of Mecca, to the places where he had received the revelations that form the basis of the historical tradition of Islam, and to sites associated with the stories of earlier figures such as Ibrahim. This 'farewell pilgrimage' is re-enacted each year in the *hajj*. As such, Muslim pilgrims to Mecca are returning to the roots of their faith and retracing the actions of those who established the path they follow.

This replication of footsteps is not always historically grounded. According to popular belief, the Shikoku pilgrimage in Japan follows the path around the island taken by the holy miracle working Buddhist figure, Kōbō Daishi. Kōbō Daishi is the posthumous name of the monk Kūkai (774–835) who was born on Shikoku and who transcended death to become a wandering miracle worker, Kōbō Daishi, who established temples and created the pilgrimage route on the island of his birth. While the story is a legend, the images it creates—of the pilgrimage as a journey following the path and in the company of the holy figure, and of his presence as the reason why the route and temples are holy—remain potent in the framework of the pilgrimage. They also provide a unifying factor between the route and temples.

Apparitions and intercessions

Often the sense of the extraordinary associated with sites of pilgrimage comes not from geography or the presence of holy founders, but from apparitions from another realm. The origins of the shrine at Lourdes centre on beliefs that the Virgin Mary appeared there to a teenage girl, Bernadette, and helped her find a spring of water that contained curative properties, thereby making Lourdes into a place specially empowered by Mary's presence and where, it was believed, her grace could be encountered. Miraculous healing stories centred on those who took the waters further advanced Lourdes' appeal and helped draw pilgrims there.

Many pilgrimage sites are similarly associated with apparitions and miracle tales. Mary is especially ubiquitous in Catholic contexts, with numerous shrines worldwide, such as Knock, Medjugorje, and Guadalupe, having their own apparition and miracle stories. Apparitions are also a formative element in many Japanese Buddhist pilgrimages. Stories of Kannon interceding to save people in distress provide the foundation legends of many temples and pilgrimages, notably the Saikoku pilgrimage, which incorporates thirty-three temples dedicated to Kannon and with stories of her miraculous apparitions, in the region around the ancient capitals of Nara and Kyoto. The Saikoku pilgrimage is, along with Shikoku, Japan's best-known and historically most significant Buddhist pilgrimage.

Saints, tombs, and relics

Relics are another phenomenon associated with the creation and development of pilgrimage cults. Beliefs that the physical traces of saints and other such figures—such as their bones, tombs, or items associated with their lives or their suffering (such as the cross on which Jesus was crucified)—contained their spiritual power and that such figures were, in effect, still alive and able to radiate grace and benefits through them, are widely found in religious contexts. Visiting a tomb thus enables people to draw close to, encounter, and commune with the holy figure interred therein, in a direct, intimate, and personal way.

In Catholicism the tombs and relics (whether actual or rumoured) of saints have been a frequent lure drawing pilgrims to specific locales. The origins of the Santiago de Compostela pilgrimage, and the sanctification of the place itself, are located in the miraculous appearance, according to legend, of the relics of St James the Apostle and martyr, on the north-east coast of Spain in the 9th century. At Padua in Italy, the Basilica of St Anthony, built after the saint's death there in the 13th century, contains his tomb, while some of his relics, including his tongue, are kept there in a reliquary. The basilica receives a steady flow of pilgrims who come to pay homage to and seek graces from the saint. They can also can purchase, from the basilica shop, small 'relics' made of muslin that have been sacralized by being passed over the tongue; the reliquary is opened occasionally for this purpose and the cloth thus sacralized is cut into small pieces for the pilgrims to take home.

Relics have frequently become the focal point of important Buddhist pilgrimages, as was seen in Chapter 1 with such examples as Sri Lanka's Temple of the Tooth. Saints' tombs are also an important focus of pilgrimage activities in other traditions. They are, for example, the focus of popular devotional pilgrimage in the Jewish tradition, while the tombs of Muslim saints such as Moinuddin Chishti at Ajmer, India, mentioned in Chapter 1, are also centres of pilgrimage activity.

So important have relics been as a means of attracting pilgrims and in making shrines into significant pilgrimage sites, that a considerable trade has developed in them in many religious traditions including Christianity and Buddhism. Pilgrims and crusaders to the Christian Holy Land frequently brought back relics they had gathered there, leading to a flood of relics—and the development of new pilgrimages to the places that acquired them—across medieval Europe. This at times impacted on other pilgrimage sites. Among the relics brought back were several purportedly of St James that were enshrined in various places such as Paris in France and Namur in Belgium, with the result that people no longer needed to travel to Santiago to visit the saint, as he had become present closer by.

Relics were stolen for such reasons. In early and medieval Christian contexts, since relics were believed to be 'alive' with the power of the saints they came from, it was believed that one could only move a relic if the saint sanctioned it. Thus if one stole a relic it was with the saint's blessing and implied that the saint was unhappy with the place it was stolen from. In the mid-9th century, for example, a monk stole a relic of the French St Foy from a rival church at Agen to install in his monastery at Conques, an act that undermined the spiritual claims of Agen and enhanced those of Conques. Similar stories of relic theft and trade abound in Buddhism too, and have played a role in spreading pilgrimage cults and sites in the areas across Asia where that tradition has been active.

Buildings and statues

Places of pilgrimage do not rely on just a striking physical location, story, or narrative linking them to saints, apparitions, or the like. Almost invariably they also develop a built environment that enshrines the central facet of their spiritual allure (such as a relic or a statue representing or embodying the figure whose apparition is associated with them), provides a focus for devotions, and inspires a sense of awe in participants. This is as true for basilicas such as those built at Lourdes and Knock to accommodate their many thousands of worshippers as it is for great cathedrals at places such as Santiago, Guadalupe, and Canterbury; Buddhist temples such as the Shwedagon in Burma and Bodh Gaya's Mahabodhi temple; mosques at major Muslim pilgrimage sites; and constructions such as the Western Wall in Jerusalem. All speak of and manifest a grandeur that aims to articulate, in physical form, the spiritual potency that the place is believed to contain.

Indeed, pilgrims have frequently expressed the desire to see striking buildings that inspire awe at the sites they visit, and their demands have often played a role in constructing the built environment of sacred places. Records indicate that early pilgrims to the Christian

Holy Land expected to see imposing churches and shrines that affirmed to them the importance of the sites they were visiting. As the flow of pilgrims developed, from the 4th century CE onwards, so did the development of buildings to meet their demands and provide a visual representation of the stories the pilgrims had read in the Bible.

Pilgrims inevitably increase the revenues of sites, through their donations, offerings, and fees for ritual services, and for items such as amulets and relics. The greater the flow of pilgrims, the more pilgrimage sites can enhance their stature through their physical environment. Prominent sites, indeed, may experience extensive and continual processes of extension and aggrandisement for such reasons. When pilgrims first began to come to Santiago from the 9th century CE, the tomb and church of St James appear to have been small and humble. Continuing proselytizing activities, however, enhanced Santiago's status and led to the construction, from the 11th century onwards, of a grand cathedral intended to provide a fitting end-point to the pilgrimage. To this day it stands, with St James himself at its apex, overlooking a large and striking square where pilgrims gather at the end of their journeys.

This does not mean that pilgrimage sites have to have large or awe-inspiring buildings. Mountainous sites such as Croagh Patrick may only have a small statue or chapel at the summit; in these cases the focus is more on, for example, the mountain itself than on any building. On the Shikoku pilgrimage some of the eighty-eight temples are large and awe-inspiring complexes, notably Zentsūji, the 75th temple and birthplace of Kūkai, the historical figure venerated posthumously as Kōbō Daishi. Some temples, however, are fairly small and unprepossessing; their significance relates to their presence on the Shikoku route, and on their legendary association with Kōbō Daishi. Local pilgrimage sites, whether in Japan or elsewhere, may be small and unimposing, just a wayside shrine or chapel, for example, or a small-scale replica of a prominent shrine elsewhere.

Distance and pilgrimage

Pilgrimage is often associated with long journeys to distant famous sites, and many of the pilgrimages discussed thus far have been of this ilk. Yet it need not be, for pilgrimage is also very much a local practice. The Shikoku pilgrimage attracts pilgrims from all over Japan and, nowadays, increasingly from overseas as well, but it is also very much a local pilgrimage, deeply linked to local island culture and identity, with a long tradition of local participation. Likewise, many pilgrims to Mecca are Saudi Arabians who travel relatively short distances there from within their own country. Local pilgrimages, often replicating distant sites, can be found in many cultural contexts, from the small-scale versions of the Shikoku and Saikoku pilgrimages found throughout Japan that initially developed for the benefit of local people (especially the poor, elderly, and infirm) unable to do these longer routes, to local versions of Lourdes and famous Indian pilgrimage sites.

Sometimes such sites cater to just their local clienteles, but they may also seek to benefit from the popularity of more famous and distant ones. Local shrines and churches along or near to the Santiago pilgrim's way, for example, have over the ages tried to attract passing pilgrims to call by at them. The monastery at Conques in France, with its stolen relic of St Foy, is one example that was extremely successful in such respects in medieval times. Like many other shrines close to the Camino, it also served as a primary pilgrimage centre offering the benefits and grace of its saint to local people who might never travel as far as Santiago or other 'great' pilgrimage centres.

Groups, play, and togetherness

Although themes of devotion, encountering the divine, seeking spiritual advancement, and asking for blessings from sacred figures are activities closely associated with pilgrimage, it would be problematic to view it simply or solely through such lenses. Entertainment and tourism have been elements in pilgrimage from early on. Particularly as pilgrimages have been popularized and as sites have become more accessible, the facilities to cater to pilgrim needs and wishes have also grown. As they have done so, they have increasingly offered scope for more than austere behaviour.

The playful aspects of pilgrimage in medieval England are aptly illustrated by the pilgrims in *The Canterbury Tales*, who tell ribald tales and eat and drink well, while studies of Japanese pilgrimage guidebooks and historical records show an increasing development of restaurants and places where better-off pilgrims could enjoy themselves. As more and more pilgrims travel in the modern day, the potential for a greater emphasis on comforts and entertainment has become increasingly prevalent.

Mention of the party of pilgrims in *The Canterbury Tales* indicates another important aspect of pilgrimage. While it has important individual dimensions (personal paths of advancement and salvation, and acquiring individual blessings, for example) it can also be a very social affair, performed in groups. Frequently it is a mass participatory event, such as the *hajj* or the Kumbh Mela, that can engender collective feelings of togetherness and identity that transcend individual, local, or national boundaries. The black American Muslim convert Malcolm X, who had advocated black separatism and denounced whites as evil, is a striking example of this. In 1964 he took part in the *hajj*, an experience that changed his life and dissolved his prejudices against other ethnicities. He wrote subsequently that for the first time in his life he felt complete as a human being and that all his previous views on race had dissolved as he sensed the oneness of humanity.

Malcolm X's experience illustrates how pilgrims may develop a sense of common belonging, something that is particularly evident when groups travel together with a common purpose or set of requests to make. The Rajasthani pilgrims described by Ann Gold who travel together by bus across India on a pilgrimage to pay homage to their dead share a common purpose. Many of the groups that travel together in Shikoku consist of parishioners of a Buddhist temple led by their priest and praying for common benefits as well as for the spirits of their ancestors. Even in such groups, however, pilgrims may still be individually motivated and with their own wishes. I have travelled on group pilgrimage tours in Shikoku, and spent time on many pilgrimage buses talking to pilgrims there. Those I have talked to have generally been content to follow group schedules, travel under a group banner and chant their prayers together. They also regularly made it clear to me that they had particular individual aims and saw their pilgrimages in distinctly personal terms.

Contest, conflict, politics, and identity

Despite such themes of collective belonging and experiences of universal harmony evident in accounts such as Malcolm X's, it would be misleading to portray pilgrimage as a practice invariably involved with harmony and togetherness. Studies by the anthropologist Michael Sallnow among Peruvian Andean Indians in the 1980s showed that their pilgrimage sites could be places of contest as different pilgrim groups jostled and competed with each other for position at shrines and sought to enhance their status over and against others. Pilgrimage parties can behave similarly in Shikoku as they seek to get better positions from which to offer their prayers before temples, or to get their pilgrimage scrolls stamped by the temple priests, while individual pilgrims might engage in games of one-upmanship about the numbers of times they have done the pilgrimage.

Reports of conflicts between different groups of pilgrims, especially when they come from different sectarian branches of Islam, sometimes surface during the *hajj*, not least among pilgrims from countries affected by political conflict, as was the case during the Iran–Iraq War of the 1980s. Such conflicts arise, too, when different faiths each claim a place as a sacred site of pilgrimage or when factions compete for control of particular sites. Jerusalem is not just a place of conflicting claims between Christians, Jews, and Muslims, for example; interdenominational conflicts also frequently surface there within these traditions. The Church of the Holy Sepulchre, seen by many as the location of Jesus's burial and resurrection, is particularly contentious, with six different Christian traditions sharing rights over the church complex, and not infrequently coming to blows over perceived violations of these rights. Kataragama in Sri Lanka is another example of a contested site where different faith and ethnic groups come on pilgrimage in ways that can produce rather then reduce tension.

Pilgrimage may also be oriented around protest, conflict, and political campaigns, as well as warfare. Catholic Church authorities such as Pope Urban II who promoted the Crusades from the late 11th century onwards, saw these campaigns as a form of pilgrimage aimed at re-imposing Christian dominance over the Christian Holy Land. Over the centuries the Santiago de Compostela pilgrimage has had powerful political and military dimensions, utilized in medieval times by the Catholic Church and Spanish monarchic forces to support the campaign to overturn Moorish Islamic control of the Iberian peninsula. Pilgrims were viewed by such agencies not simply as people walking to Santiago to encounter St James. They were foot soldiers in the *reconquista*, the campaign to drive out the Moors and unify the peninsula under a Christian banner. St James was adopted under the guise of Santiago Matamaros ('St James the Moorslayer') as the patron saint of this campaign.

Pilgrimage sites are often associated with affirmations of national and ethnic identities, and as a means of expressing opposition to other identity groups. The image of Mary in the Basilica of Our Lady of Guadalupe in Mexico is not simply a focus of devotional pilgrimages; she is also a symbol of Mexican unity and identity. Stories of the initial apparitions at Guadalupe, said to have occurred in 1531, claim that Mary spoke in the local language rather than that of the Spanish conquerors who had recently brought Catholicism to the region. This meant that as the Marian cult of pilgrimage developed at Guadalupe, it took on a specifically ethnic dimension, allowing the indigenous population to develop their own form of Christian identity and association with Mary, separate from (and implicitly superior to) the conquering Spaniards. In later ages, too, armies fighting for Mexican independence often marched under the banner of Guadalupe's Marian image.

Pilgrimages continue to be utilized for political purposes in modern times. In 1990, Lal Advani, the leader of the Hindu nationalist Bharatiya Janata Party (BJP), led followers on a *rath yatra* or 'chariot pilgrimage' from Somnath temple in Gujarat to Ayodhya in northern India, claimed by Hindus as the birthplace of the deity Ram. The vehicles used in the pilgrimage, decked out with images of Ram, were referred to as chariots because that is Ram's vehicle in Hindu legends. The aim of the 'chariot pilgrimage' was to reclaim a piece of land, occupied by a mosque, that Hindu nationalists said was Ram's birthplace. The pilgrimage paved the way for the later violent destruction of the mosque by Hindu militants in 1992, while advancing the BJP's political Hindu nationalist agenda.

Tombs also can be highly controversial pilgrimage sites tinged with political, nationalist, and extreme religious attitudes. This was illustrated clearly after the American Jewish extremist Baruch Goldstein massacred twenty-nine Palestinian Muslims at a mosque in Hebron on the West Bank in 1994. Goldstein's agenda appears to have been to kill as many Muslims as possible to stop them hindering Jewish settlement (which Goldstein saw as sanctioned by God) of the region. Goldstein was beaten to death by the Palestinians who stopped his murder spree, and was buried in the Israeli-held West Bank. Shortly afterwards his tomb was adorned with a shrine and prayer area and turned into a pilgrimage site by Jewish extremists who viewed his deed as a sacred act for the sake of Israel. Eventually to forestall such activity, the Israeli Army destroyed the shrine area in 1999, although the tomb continues to draw visitors.

Common themes

In essence pilgrimage incorporates three main elements: travel and movement, veneration in some form, and a special place or places considered to have some deep significance (often associated with sacred figures or founders) that makes them stand out from the world around them. Similarly those who perform pilgrimages—pilgrims—are people who travel to and perform acts of meaningful significance such as praying and performing rituals at and on the route to such special places. These may be built places (churches, temples, shrines, tombs) as well as natural features (such as mountains, caves, and river-crossing places), although usually such locations, too, are marked out by physical buildings that have been built there.

What remains constant is the notion of people making their way to and seeking to be in such places, in the ambit of the special figures associated with them. The journey can have both real and symbolic meanings: movement to a physical place and metaphorical journeying to a spiritual destination. Pilgrimage thus can be universal in meanings as well as highly localized. Within this framework pilgrimage can provide the setting for expressions of individual development and self-awareness along with group-related senses of togetherness and belonging, and yet also provide potential for contest and conflict. In such ways pilgrimage encompasses a wide variety of themes and meanings, frequently dependent on individual interpretations and volition, that are sometimes (for instance, in simultaneously offering pilgrims scope for a sense of communal harmony and a means of expressing difference) contradictory. It is this complex richness of potentialities and scope that is so central to its appeal and to the seemingly simple act of leaving one's normal life and, as the Latin term expresses it, 'going through the fields'.

Chapter 3
More than miracles

While miraculous tales, apparitions, associations with religious leaders, the claimed presence of deities, and striking geographical features may all be important elements in pilgrimages, their presence does not automatically mean that the places where they occur will become flourishing pilgrimage sites. Issues of accessibility along with the ways in which various interest groups promote and support the development of pilgrimage cults, are also significant factors. Here we will look at a number of well-known sites around the world to learn more about their emergence and to see how important practical considerations played a role in their development.

Lourdes, miracles, and trains

In 1858 the teenage Bernadette Soubirous had a series of visions in which a lady appeared to her near her home in Lourdes, southern France, told her to pray for sinners, and revealed to her a spring of water. The 'lady' was the Virgin Mary and quickly rumours spread that praying to her at Lourdes and imbibing the spring waters there could heal illness and help the afflicted. Yet, while the apparitions along with Bernadette's saintly image and popular beliefs about the healing qualities of the spring water were central to the appeal of Lourdes, other factors were also significant in the transformation of the town into one of the world's most famous pilgrimage sites.

The apparitions occurred in an era when the French state was promoting anti-clerical secularist policies. Although church authorities were reluctant to support outbursts of popular piety, fearing these might tar the church with accusations of superstition and backwardness in an era that emphasized education and rationalism, they saw in the Lourdes apparitions and miracle stories a chance to resist this secular turn. Bernadette's sincere and devout nature was particularly useful in this respect, and within four years of the apparitions Lourdes was declared an official Catholic pilgrimage site.

Local civic authorities and entrepreneurs also played their part. At a time when the local economy was in decline, the apparitions presented opportunities for regenerating Lourdes. Local businesses began producing goods to sell to pilgrims, ranging from statuettes of Mary, to souvenirs, postcards, and Pastilles de Lourdes (lozenges of sugar and grotto water attributed with healing properties). Enterprises sending Lourdes water in bottles to distant destinations, such as the USA, further extended Lourdes' reputation, while civic authorities developed an infrastructure of information, publicity, and affordable accommodation that made Lourdes accessible to the less well-off. The opening of a railway line in 1866 linking Lourdes to the national railway network brought it within the ambit of people from afar. French Railways publicized pilgrimages to Lourdes to encourage use of the new rail system, and church authorities further increased Lourdes' popularity by laying on special train pilgrimages from Paris and elsewhere.

Church support, local entrepreneurialism, and advantageous transport links thus were significant in transforming Lourdes into a national and international pilgrimage centre. Its rise was not without controversy, however. Critics attacked its populist piety and miracle stories as examples of the superstition that they hoped would be eradicated by education and secularism. They were particularly hostile towards the selling of souvenirs and religious trinkets around the shrine, seeing them as tacky and crassly commercial—issues that Lourdes became something of a byword for. Church authorities, too, were concerned about this and, fearing that the Lourdes souvenir trade would give Catholicism a bad name, tried (not always successfully) to control such sales while maintaining a separation between the grotto area and the shops. They were cautious about what to officially sanction as miracles, with the institute established to examine miracle claims ratifying fewer than seventy of the many stories of miraculous healing that have emerged at the site since the 1860s. Such caution is intended to ensure that Catholic authorities retained control of the Lourdes cult rather than let it be swamped by populist enthusiasm.

Pilgrim numbers grew rapidly until, nowadays, Lourdes gets more than six million visitors a year, some coming back each year (see Figure 7). Pilgrims have not been daunted by church reluctance to officially recognize the many miracle tales that circulate among them or by Lourdes' apparent commercialism. The souvenir shops attacked by critics have been a continuing attraction, while Lourdes remains a symbol of promise, hope, and devotion. The unwell hope to alleviate bodily suffering, while healthy devotees come not just to worship and shop but as volunteers accompanying the sick and helping them bathe in the waters. Many visit in faith groups, which include the healthy and the infirm, organized by local dioceses in their home countries. Their focus is primarily on the actions, bathing, and prayers they perform at Lourdes, more than on the journeys there (often these days by plane). In such ways Lourdes is a site centred on practices and events at a specific place where stories of miracle and apparition enhanced by entrepreneurial acumen, local civic support, and good transport links have created a powerful pilgrimage culture.

7. **Pilgrimage group, with helpers and people in wheelchairs, in front of the Basilica at Lourdes.**

The Camino, relics, and publicity

If Lourdes focuses on place, the Santiago de Compostela pilgrimage incorporates the notion of a route: the Camino that leads to a specific sacred goal, the cathedral at Santiago. Its reputation developed thanks to tales of miraculous events along with the promotional efforts of ecclesiastical agencies that made a remote corner of Galicia into a major pilgrimage location. According to Santiago legends, St James (Santiago) the Apostle visited Spain to spread Christianity, while after martyrdom in 44 CE his relics were secretly taken there, to be miraculously rediscovered at Santiago in 813. Santiago's bishop, Teodomiro, affirmed the validity of the relics and a church was constructed to house them.

Pilgrimage provided an opportunity for adventure and Santiago and its Apostolic relics—distant and exotic for much of Europe but not as far or dangerous to reach as Jerusalem—proved attractive

to those driven by faith and the wish to see distant places. Stories
of St James's miraculous aid to pilgrims provided further incentive.
Vigorous promotion by Church officials, notably the 12th century
bishop Diego Gelmírez, who had close links to the Vatican and
travelled widely, promoting pilgrimages to his cathedral, along
with the adoption of St James as patron saint of the campaign to
reassert Christian and Hispanic control over Iberia, furthered
the cause. As did the Cluniac Benedictine order: keen to expand
its influence and extend the political frontiers of Christendom,
it used its monastic networks to promote Santiago throughout
Europe; organized pilgrimages there; and offered accommodation
for pilgrims along the way. Papal declarations of Holy Years
when pilgrimages to Santiago would bring the remission of
sins also helped.

Several routes developed across Europe to Santiago; the *Codex
Calixtinus* (a 12th century collection of documents about the
pilgrimage) lists four from France, including one from Paris,
where the Tour St Jacques still marks the beginning of this route.
The routes were difficult, through the Pyrenees, across Spain,
and taking many weeks to walk. The *Codex* warns about brigands,
wild dogs, and people who will cheat pilgrims, but it also offers
hopes of miracles by St James and portrays pilgrims as holy
figures entitled to alms and good treatment from those they met.
Some came by sea, notably English pilgrims, who took boats
from southern English ports to northern Spain, thereby shortening
the distance they had to walk. Many medieval pilgrims were
poor, sick, and seeking cures. Some were doing it as penance or
to seek remission of sins. All were aware that death was a real
danger, while believing that dying on pilgrimage would grant
them salvation.

The pilgrimage went into decline from the 17th century as
alternative pilgrimage places and possibilities of adventure
appeared. Also the 'reconquest' of Iberia, completed in 1492, reduced
the allure of its earlier position on the borders of Christendom.

Pilgrim numbers were virtually nil in the 19th century until, in 1884, Pope Leo XIII reaffirmed the validity of the relics, and instigated new campaigns to promote them. In the mid-20th century the Spanish dictator General Franco, a native of Galicia where Santiago is located, took up the mantle and further promoted the city by encouraging pilgrimages there as a way of promoting the muscular Spanish Catholic nationalism that helped underpin his brutal regime.

As Spain was democratized after Franco's death in 1975 authorities began to emphasize the pilgrimage's cultural significance while diminishing its earlier emphasis on Catholic nationalism. The Spanish government included Santiago in a list of places to promote as sites of heritage tourism, while regional Galician government campaigns to increase tourism advertised the pilgrimage in order to attract people to the region. International accolades, including UNESCO World Heritage status for the city (1985) and pilgrimage (1993), and the Camino's selection by the Council of Europe as the first European Cultural Itinerary, further enhanced its reputation and increased pilgrim numbers. So did the Catholic Church's declaration of Holy Years in 1993, 1999, and 2010, when pilgrims were offered remission for sins; in these years pilgrimage mascots were also created to publicize the pilgrimage. The 2010 mascot, Xubi, even has its own Twitter account, and features widely on posters and other Santiago publicity.

Pilgrim numbers have risen considerably in recent years, particularly those of walkers, while well-known books by people such as Hape Kerkeling, Paulo Coelho, and Shirley MacLaine have added to this process. The result of this contemporary growth is that while some of those who walk along the Camino state they are Catholics, a significant number refute any affiliation to organized religion, stating they are motivated by a sense of personal challenge and spiritual search, often articulating their views in New Age terms. Some see walking the Camino as the opportunity for a long-distance hike linked to notions of European cultural unity and shared values. Cheap places to stay and support structures provided by regional authorities (which now publicize the Camino as a holiday destination for hikers) have made the route very affordable, thereby further increasing its appeal, while (in the eyes of some) turning it increasingly into a hiking route as much as a path of pilgrimage.

The Santiago pilgrimage thus shows how ecclesiastical, political, and, in modern times, cultural and tourist authorities, have played major roles in developing, reviving, and expanding the pilgrimage clientele. At the same time changes in the orientations of pilgrims have occurred. For medieval pilgrims, their journeys tended to be underpinned by notions of fighting for Christendom and were performed with hopes of healing and the eradication of sins. Contemporary pilgrims, on the other hand, may well eschew any overt associations with faith and religion and see their pilgrimages more through the lenses of personalized spiritual search, the challenge of hiking and issues of cultural identity. Observers at the traditional daily pilgrim's mass at Santiago in modern times have noted more of an emphasis on cameras and commemorative photographs than on prayer and piety. Yet even if the medieval notions of piety are not as prominent as in earlier times, many pilgrims continue to come to Santiago not by convenient modern modes of transport available to them, but on foot, in the manner and along the routes trodden by pilgrims of earlier times.

Shikoku: walking with a holy figure

While the Santiago pilgrims follow a linear route watched over by a saint, pilgrims in Shikoku go on a circuit involving eighty-eight temples that have to be visited in order to complete the pilgrimage. They, too, are guarded by a sacred figure as they travel. Their white pilgrim shirts are inscribed with an image of Kōbō Daishi and with Japanese ideograms indicating the phrase 'two pilgrims together' (*dōgyōninin*) signifying that each pilgrim is accompanied by Kōbō Daishi.

There are no reliable records of when the pilgrimage began or why it has eighty-eight temples. Evidence suggests that from around the 12th century Buddhist monks began visiting the island where Kūkai, the human precursor of the miracle-working Kōbō Daishi, was born, to visit places where he had performed austerities and walk in his footsteps. A route with eighty-eight temples around the island coalesced over some centuries as a result of such travels. The first records of a pilgrimage with that number of sites date from the mid-17th century, with the temples numbered in the most convenient order to circle the island from what, in that era, was its main port of entry. Such records, however, provide no evidence to indicate why there are eighty-eight temples.

Records show that most pilgrims were poor and sought help from Kōbō Daishi in the face of diseases and suffering. Early Shikoku miracle tale collections talk of intercession, salvation, and the eradication of sins, and promise that pilgrims will meet Kōbō Daishi along the way and receive his grace. Pilgrims (mostly male until the advent of modern transport) walked for lack of any alternative, often sleeping rough or dependent on local hospitality because of their poverty. Many received support from local people, for Shikoku islanders have long supported pilgrims through giving them alms, a practice that in local pilgrimage terms is believed to allow the donor to share in the merits of the pilgrimage.

While many pilgrims travel together in groups and others walk alone, they are all linked together by the pilgrimage's core common symbols. The notion of being together with Kōbō Daishi means that no pilgrim is ever alone; it also means they are united together through their shared association with him. The pilgrimage as a symbolic journey to enlightenment and as a journey in another realm, with pilgrims dressed for death and travelling in its realms, are important uniting themes. Such images remain potent even if nowadays, with safe bus tours and modern facilities, death is no longer the ever-present threat of past ages.

Whenever new developments made the route easier, pilgrims used them, from bridges and ferries across inlets and rivers in the 18th century, to the trains and buses that have become common in the present era. The development of bus package tour pilgrimages from the 1950s has particularly boosted pilgrim numbers and increased access to greater numbers of people, while Japan's economic development has provided more people with the financial ability to travel more widely. Pilgrims today can choose many ways to make their pilgrimages; while bus tours are most common, increasingly people are going by car, while others walk or use a mixture of cars, trains, and other means. There is no fixed route, for one can start and finish anywhere, and one can even do the pilgrimage in sections. The one stipulation is to visit all eighty-eight temples at some point. During the 1980s, with the rise of bus tours and the use of cars, foot pilgrims became rare; during the forty days that my wife and I spent on the pilgrimage route in 1984 we saw only half a dozen other foot pilgrims. Since the 1990s, however, walkers have again become prominent. Many of them are older men who lost their jobs in Japan's 1990s recession and who walk the pilgrimage to 'find themselves' while confronting the emotional problems of unemployment. Others are young people interested in hiking, seeking personal challenges, and espousing New Age ideas of spiritual search while saying they have no interest in Buddhism or organized religion.

Modern developments have boosted pilgrim numbers from a few thousand in the 1950s to well over 100,000 a year today. Another factor in its contemporary popularity is that (similar to the Santiago pilgrimage's associations with European cultural heritage) the Shikoku pilgrimage is widely regarded in Japan nowadays not so much as a Buddhist pilgrimage, but as one associated with Japanese heritage and cultural traditions. This linkage has been fostered by various documentaries produced about the pilgrimage, as well as by the publicity, guidebooks, and, more recently, internet sites, produced by the pilgrimage temples and by regional travel companies, government agencies, and tourist offices for whom the pilgrimage is an important aspect of the local economy. Such interest groups have worked closely with the temples to promote the pilgrimage and to develop increasingly comfortable facilities for pilgrims. All of this has increased the pilgrimage's appeal, especially to older Japanese people from the big cities, who see in the slower, more rural nature of Shikoku, nostalgic resonances of an older, more traditional Japan, and for whom the pilgrimage thus can serve as a journey through their cultural heritage and past as well as providing a way of expressing faith.

Mecca and the *hajj*

Compared to Santiago and Shikoku, where pilgrims need no prior religious affiliation (and may proclaim a lack of it), pilgrimages to Mecca are restricted only to those who are Muslims. They involve journeying to the epicentre of a world religion, where, in Islamic belief, awareness of monotheism began and where Allah's revelations to Mohammed led to the establishment of a formal tradition. Pilgrimages can be made all year round, but the peak period is the eighth to thirteenth days of the twelfth month of the Muslim (lunar) year: the time of the *hajj*. Performing it is one of Islam's five pillars of faith, something all Muslims should do unless they are prevented from doing so by special circumstances (e.g. poverty, age, or infirmity).

In eras past the route to Mecca was dangerous, with numerous records of pilgrims dying of thirst in the deserts of Arabia, drowning in barely seaworthy boats crossing to the Arabian peninsula, or being stricken by epidemics and outbreaks of cholera. From the late 19th century better transport and health facilities made the journey quicker and safer. The most dramatic modern change is air travel; previously a Muslim in Indonesia, for example, would have to undergo a long, fraught journey to reach Mecca (and get home again) that might take years. Now she/he can do it in a matter of hours. In the 1930s there were around 30,000 *hajj* pilgrims per year; now it is over two million, who mostly travel by plane.

Improving economic conditions, including oil wealth, have provided resources to allow more people to travel, as has the expansion of pilgrim support facilities provided by the Saudi Arabian regime, which uses its control of Islam's holiest sites and the pilgrimage to boost its authority. Saudi authorities regulate the numbers of pilgrims by allocating annual pilgrim quotas to each country, because the numbers of pilgrims that can be managed during the *hajj* period is finite. Such quotas ensure that Muslims from around the globe can participate, but they also are a means through which the Saudi regime is able to heighten its influence over other Muslim countries. The US-based Moroccan scholar Abdellah Hammoudi, for example, was required to apply for registration among the pilgrim quota in his native Morocco and join a package tour arranged by Saudi travel companies in order to participate in the 1999 *hajj*.

The emphasis is on the ritual processes carried out around Mecca and Medina. Pilgrims theoretically are equal; all wear special white clothing, made up of two sheets, that signifies ritual purity (*ihram*) and indicates that all are the same on pilgrimage. They usually bring the *ihram* cloth home afterwards and may (similarly to Shikoku pilgrims) use it as a burial shroud at death. The pilgrimage expresses key themes and stories of the tradition that are ritually re-enacted as the faithful replicate the footsteps and actions of their prophets. Mass participation means that all are performing these actions together, thereby expressing a sense of unity together via a universal ritual language of belonging.

During the rituals (usually led by pilgrimage guides, *mutawwif*), pilgrims express complete surrender to Allah, circle the Ka'aba seven times, and, at one point, run seven times (in all, three and a half kilometres) between two hills where Ibrahim's bondswoman Hagar is said to have run seeking water while abandoned in the desert. Because this ritual has taken its toll on pilgrims in the desert heat, Saudi authorities have now constructed air-conditioned tunnels for the purpose—one of several steps towards making the pilgrimage more convenient and enabling vast crowds to move speedily through the ritual cycle. At the end of the *hajj* there is a mass communal feast in which sheep are purchased, slaughtered, offered to Allah, and eaten. While those who cannot afford it are not obliged to buy a sheep, the well-off are expected to do so and to share it with their less well-off fellow pilgrims.

The *hajj* thus emphasizes unity, solidarity, and fellowship, along with origins, enabling pilgrims to walk in the footsteps of their prophets and reiterate their deeds. It emphasizes ideals of ritual purity and serves as a declaration of faith. It also provides participants with an enhancement of status within their communities, for all who make the *hajj* can take the title *hajji* to distinguish themselves thereafter.

The pilgrimage is not free of tensions or controversy. The potential for conflict between different factions or national groups was mentioned in Chapter 1. The control exerted by the Saudi regime grates with some. The increasing emphasis on making the pilgrimage more convenient, while enabling more pilgrims than ever to visit Mecca, causes pilgrims to complain that they are harried into performing devotions quickly and moving on to let the next throng through, and that areas within the sacred arena have been turned into huge bus parking lots. Massive building programmes have controversially demolished Mecca's older historical quarters and replaced them with luxury hotels for the very rich, driving up accommodation prices and making the pilgrimage more difficult for the poor (see Figure 8). To some critics, too, the provision of luxury hotels where rich pilgrims can dine out overlooking the Ka'aba, while also being provided with all manner of opulent services—including spa treatments and personal butlers to deal with their every wish—runs counter to the egalitarianism symbolized by the simple pilgrimage clothes worn during the *hajj*.

In such ways the *hajj* manifests an extraordinary blend of universal themes, of piety, practice, equality, purity, ritual re-enactment, and

54

8. Mecca: pilgrims, the Kaʾaba, and surrounding hotels.

reaffirmation of foundation stories, along with themes of
control, mechanization, commerce, and increasing opulence.
It not only manifests how a great religion can place pilgrimage
at its core, but also how modern developments have expanded
pilgrim numbers and enhanced the commercial dimensions of
the pilgrimage.

Two Indian pilgrimage sites

In northern India two Hindu pilgrimage sites—Hardwar and Shri Mata Vaishno Devi temple—illustrate how geography, landscape, and legends provide the basis for the development of pilgrimage sites. They are also examples of how factors such as transport facilities and skilled promotion can transform places with relatively local clienteles into major national pilgrimage centres with millions of visitors.

Hardwar's religious significance comes from its position at one of Ganges' most sacred points, where it emerges from the mountains into the north Indian plains. Various myths and Hindu texts indicate the spiritual presence there of Hindu deities, notably Shiva, who is closely associated with the Ganges. Bathing at Hardwar and performing rituals for the deceased there form significant elements in its standing as a pilgrimage centre. Hardwar also hosts the Kumbh Mela (which occurs every three years at one of four sites in India) every twelve years.

While myths indicating the spiritual presence of deities such as Shiva along with its position on the Ganges clearly mark Hardwar out as a significant place for rituals and spiritual devotions, historical records indicate that until the 19th century it did not attract many pilgrims from beyond its region. Thereafter a variety of social, cultural, and political processes widened its appeal. These included investment in the town to improve its economy, the building of new riverside bathing areas and temples, and the activities of Hardwar's ritual specialists, who assiduously promoted their site and developed services and facilities for increasing numbers of pilgrims. Importantly, too, improvements in health facilities that (as at Mecca) made visiting in large crowds safer through the control of diseases such as cholera, along with the opening of a railway line to Hardwar in 1886, had a major impact. The railway in particular transformed Hardwar from a pilgrimage site only accessible to people living relatively close by or prepared to make long and arduous, potentially life-threatening journeys there, to a place reachable from across the country in comparatively short time. Indian Railways helped in this process by encouraging people from across the country to develop a sense of national identity by visiting places of national significance such as pilgrimage sites. Through seeking to increase public use of the rail network, the railways thus became avid supporters and promoters of pilgrimage sites such as Hardwar.

This is not to attribute Hardwar's development simply to modern conveniences or non-religious factors. Its standing in Hindu myths and its geographical setting as a crossing and bathing place of immense significance on the holiest of Indian rivers remain fundamental. People visit Hardwar because of its religious significance: in order to bathe, seek favour with the gods, and perform rituals for the dead. Their focus is on the practices performed at the sacred site itself, rather than on the manner of getting there. What developments such as the railways have done is to expand the scope of Hardwar and to make it a nationally accessible pilgrimage centre, so that Hindus from all over the nation can become pilgrims there.

Shri Mata Vaishno Devi temple in the foothills of Jammu received around 30,000 pilgrims a year in the 1940s; by 2007 the number was seven and a half million. It is an example of how a place can rapidly become a highly successful pilgrimage site in the modern day and of how modern secular government policies may contribute to this process.

Similar to Amarnath, this is a shrine centred on a cave in the hills, although lower, at just over 1,600 metres, than Amarnath. It involves a twelve-kilometre hike up to the cave where Mata Vaishno Devi (the Mother Goddess) resides and where her spiritual powers may be accessed. Traditionally one of seven goddess shrines, known as the Seven Sisters, in the Siwālik region of Jammu, its myths associate the cave with a powerful female deity who, having subjugated evil-doers, retreated there to meditate. She assumed the form of the rocks within the cave, where a natural rock formation with three protrusions, known as pindies, signifies her presence. The pindies are the focus of pilgrims, who come seeking the goddess's *darshan* (seeing/revering a spiritual presence, which projects grace onto the seer) and pray for her divine help. Her reputation as a protector of the poor and as a granter of boons attracted a stream of pilgrims from within the region, although at relatively low levels until the 1970s, when shrine authorities began improving conditions to enable the site to receive around 5,000 pilgrims a day.

New roads coupled with the passing of the Shri Mata Vaishno Devi Shrine Act in 1986 by the regional government proved significant. The Act was controversial in its intention of reforming shrine management (deemed by the state to be corrupt), but it also sought to generate more pilgrims, improve access, accommodation facilities, and other support facilities, including good drinking water, post offices, banks, shops, and police stations. These made the area around the shrine more accessible and the experience of visiting and trekking up to the shrine less arduous. Intensive promotional activities by the shrine authorities and by the regional government, for which the shrine has become an important generator of revenues and source of jobs in the pilgrim support industry, have added to the shrine's stature. Shrine and government publicity, via mass media advertisements and internet sites promoting the spiritual benefits of worshipping at the shrine and its accessibility (thereby encouraging people from all walks of life that they can manage to do the pilgrimage), has made the shrine widely known not just in northern India but throughout the country.

Accessibility (as at Amarnath) now includes the possibility of flying in via helicopter tours arranged through the shrine, although that is something only the relatively wealthy can afford. Pilgrim growth has been such that the shrine now far outstrips its 'Sisters' (which have not had the benefit of such infrastructure support) as a pilgrimage centre. Such growth has, as at Mecca and elsewhere, led to its problems, with numbers so great that authorities have now had to start regulating pilgrim numbers and restricting the time pilgrims can spend in the cave for their *darshan* to under a minute.

Such developments have impacted on the profile of pilgrims, transforming it from a regional to a national shrine with an increasing emphasis on middle-class pilgrims from urban areas (particularly since the goddess is said to look kindly on prayers for economic betterment). The growth has not impressed all, whether because the crowds make it difficult to spend long in the deity's presence or because there are (as at other sites we have encountered) those who regard austere travel and hardship as important elements in gaining the deity's favour.

This does not mean that the pilgrimage is easy or simply one that has been transformed by comforts. Pilgrims generally still have to trek the last twelve kilometres up to the shrine from the nearest transport facilities, unless they use helicopter services that are, in theory, for those unable to manage the hike. The shrine's religious appeal lies in its goddess, her myths, the cave where her presence can be felt and seen through the pindies, and the benefits she bestows on the faithful who visit her. Building on such things, state support and skilful promotion, along with the development of infrastructures to help pilgrims, have played a significant part in raising its standing so that it now receives millions of pilgrims a year.

A popular folk deity in Vietnam

Bà Chúa Xù, the Lady of the Realm shrine, close to Vietnam's border with Cambodia, is another that has become extremely popular in the same period as has Shri Mata Vaishno Devi and that also exemplifies how pilgrimage sites can experience rapid bursts of popularity in accord with the times. Now the most visited shrine in Vietnam, with over a million pilgrims a year, it enshrines a female deity with eclectic roots linking popular Buddhism, folk religions, and regional influences, including from the neighbouring Khmer Cambodian tradition. The deity is believed by supplicants to have the power to bestow benefits on them, and she is especially popular with traders and merchants, particularly females, who come to pray for her support.

As Vietnam began to open up to a market economy during the 1980s, earlier restrictions on popular religiosity were loosened, thereby giving vent to an increasingly market-oriented religious culture. This was aided also by the combination of new-found wealth coupled with the uncertainties of a market economy that, while giving people increasing funds to travel, also created unease because of market vagaries. This has benefited the cults of goddesses that offer emotional assurance and worldly benefits, such as the Lady of the Realm, whose this-worldly ethos fits well with such market orientations. Located on the border with Cambodia, the Lady of the Realm also articulates notions of Vietnamese identity and affirmations of its prowess in comparison to other cultures. Stories associated with the appearance of the Lady's statue combine miraculous events in her manifestation before a local girl, with myths identifying her as a protector of Vietnamese interests against the neighbouring Cambodians.

Such themes, along with improved transport services that allow people in several of the country's major urban areas to make rapid and regular pilgrimages there to seek her benefits and simultaneously express their sense of Vietnamese identity, have been central to her rise since the 1980s. A variety of shrine events including colourful festivals have further drawn in crowds. As with other pilgrimage sites mentioned here, there are also tensions around the shrine. The rural local people see the goddess as a protector of local interests and moral values that are not shared by those who come as pilgrims from urban areas, and whom locals

60

view as being motivated by mercenary interests and by the Lady's ability to bestow worldly benefits. Similarly the exuberant festivals that draw pilgrims to the shrine are largely attended by locals, for whom the fun is part and parcel of the dynamics of their shrine, while urban and town dwellers are more likely to disparage the frivolity of festival times, viewing them as the domain of country 'hicks' and making their own pilgrimages outside of the festive periods.

Popularity, growth, and modern impulses

While the previous examples outlining the histories and/or the modern processes of development and popularity of a small number of pilgrimage sites are not exhaustive, they are illustrative of some common patterns and themes in pilgrimage contexts. They inform us that when pilgrimages attract crowds of people, especially over extended periods, a complex amalgam of factors is involved. A common image of pilgrimage development relates to the idea of miraculous events such as apparitions and cures of illness, themes evident, for example, at Lourdes, as crucial. Another centres on the role of religious leaders, saints, and other such figures in creating or producing paths for others to follow and through which core values and symbolic meanings may be expressed.

Generally, however, more mundane factors are also involved, and are highly important, in pilgrimage development and success. They include the activities of religious proselytisers such as Bishop Gelmírez with his campaigns to put Santiago on the Christian map, and political factors, such as the support of regional and civic agencies, as seen at Shri Mata Vaishno Devi, the promotional help given to the Shikoku pilgrimage by regional agencies, and the various ways in which regional and political forces have sought to use, support, develop, and publicize the Santiago pilgrimage. Regional and local factors of identity and changing socio-economic conditions can play their part, as with the post-Communist, economically liberalizing Vietnam's example of a local folklore deity that has attained national status and attracts a clientele associated with that country's socio-economic changes, increasing mobility and concerns for identity. Concepts of global religious identity and localized political control, as in the *hajj*, also may be factors behind recent growth in particular contexts.

Running through all these examples is a recurrent influence of modernization and its concomitants such as the development of modern transport systems that speed up travel, open sites up to greater population hinterlands, and transform places that once relied on a predominantly local and regional clientele into national and international pilgrimage sites. This informs us that in examining why certain places become highly visible on the pilgrimage map one has to pay attention to more than just their foundation stories associated with miracles, apparitions, and sacred deeds, ritual re-enactments, and spiritual and worldly rewards. While these may be important initial factors, they invariably require something else if the places they are associated with are to become more than localized and temporarily popular places. It is when interest groups that may not necessarily be religious in organization, commercial organizations, convenient transport facilities, and other such factors coalesce together that places associated with miraculous stories and apparitions are able to develop into vibrant centres of pilgrimage that endure and attract pilgrims from far and wide.

Chapter 4
Practices, motives, and experiences

At the Greek Orthodox Church of the Madonna of the Annunciation on the Aegean island of Tinos some pilgrims crawl on their hands and knees up the street and steps leading to the shrine, perhaps because they have made a special vow to show their devotion in this way or because they feel that such public demonstrations of piety enhance the petitions they make to the Madonna. They may also endure hardships on the island if they cannot afford a bed and have to sleep in the streets. Not all pilgrims make such dramatic approaches, however, for austerities are not deemed mandatory for pilgrims. Many simply walk up to the shrine and demonstrate their devotion by making monetary and other offerings. They may also stay in comfortable accommodation, while some combine their pilgrimages with a vacation on the island, visiting its beaches and going swimming.

Such scenes, in which some pilgrims engage in ascetic practices and others take more comfortable paths, are common in pilgrimage contexts. In August 1971, when I walked to Amarnath from the nearest town, Pahalagam, at the start of the annual pilgrimage season, I met many sadhus—ascetic devotees of Shiva—who wore barely any clothing, begged for alms, and viewed their pilgrimage as an ascetic journey of devotion. I also encountered better-off pilgrims who rode horses, had guides who cooked for them, and stayed overnight in tents (see Figure 9).

9. On the pilgrimage path to Amarnath, Kashmir.

Nowadays, with enhanced support facilities, including helicopter tours to shorten the trip for those who wish to pay for the privilege, the Amarnath pilgrimage displays an even greater admixture of ascetics, foot pilgrims, and the well-off using horseback and other means of transport to make their journeys less arduous. At Kataragama in Sri Lanka, Hindus and Buddhists come making supplications to the deity Murukan (known to the Buddhists as Skanda). Some engage in dramatic ascetic displays to show their devotion and sincerity, walking on hot coals, and/or engaging in self-mortifications to show the deity that they are worthy of his benevolence. Others come by bus and car and enjoy the creature comforts available around the site, to the extent that various complaints have emerged in the Sri Lankan media and elsewhere that Kataragama has become tainted by frivolous touristic behaviour.

On pilgrimage routes such as Shikoku and Santiago the picture is the same, of diverse, even seemingly contradictory, modes of pilgrimages. Pilgrims, weather-beaten and dusty after walking for many weeks, may reach the cathedral at Santiago alongside others fresh from flying in and taking taxis from the airport. In Shikoku I have met people performing the pilgrimage as an ascetic practice intended to punish and purify their bodies and to increase their spiritual awareness. In 1984 my wife and I walked for a day with a young man who was camping out, begging for alms, and living only on uncooked food. He saw his pilgrimage as an ascetic practice in which he was following in the footsteps of his spiritual teacher, who had similarly walked the pilgrimage many years before, and of mendicants of earlier ages. We also met many people travelling by car, bus, taxis, and other means of transport.

Sometimes, too, I have talked to people who view their pilgrimages in Shikoku as a holiday. On one bus tour pilgrimage I became friends with a Japanese man in his sixties who told me his hobby was photographing ancient temples and natural scenery. He wanted to visit Shikoku and a pilgrimage bus tour provided the most convenient way to get around the island; since it stopped at each temple for forty-five minutes, it gave him plenty of time to take photographs. At temple courtyards pilgrims who have spent days hiking on mountainous paths might mingle with groups travelling in modern coaches and staying in hotels with modern facilities and sumptuous food each evening.

Such pictures of contrast are not just a modern phenomenon. The merry horseback pilgrims in *The Canterbury Tales* were not an anomaly; 12th century records indicate that perhaps a third of pilgrims to Canterbury were knights and nobles, while aristocratic pilgrims, often travelling in some comfort, were widespread across Europe. They shared the route with impoverished pilgrims on foot, even as they differed in their modes of travel and expenditures. While it was common in earlier eras for pilgrims to Mecca to endure harsh conditions, there are also records of Muslim potentates making pilgrimages there in grand style. In 1324, for instance, Musa I, the Emperor of the Malian Empire in West Africa, made an extravagant pilgrimage to Mecca with a vast entourage of retainers, slaves, horses, camels, food, gold (some of which he gave to the poor he encountered), and other goods.

Contrasts and juxtapositions of gaiety and despair were also evident amongst 18th and 19th century Shikoku pilgrims. Graves along the route and temple records of pilgrims dying in their courtyards are testimony to the often precarious existence of pilgrims in earlier times. Many were poverty-stricken, dependent on alms, often sick, and desperately seeking miraculous cures. Some were afflicted with leprosy, seen at the time as a spiritual curse that caused sufferers to be driven from their homes, leaving them little choice but to wander as pilgrims begging for alms while praying for healing and salvation. Yet in the same period pilgrimages in Shikoku were also done, especially in spring, by local age-sets as an initiation rite. This also provided such young people the chance to seek out suitable partners from other villages. Thus groups of merry-making young on the lookout for partners shared the route with devout ascetics and the impoverished, sick, and dying.

Choices, complaints, and 'authenticity'

The ability to choose how to shape and perform a pilgrimage is one of its appeals. This is particularly enhanced by modern developments that offer pilgrims multiple choices of travel, unlike in earlier eras when few apart from the aristocracy and elites could do other than walk or perhaps be crammed into a boat, where levels of comfort depended on how much one could afford. Nowadays, numerous ways of doing pilgrimages are widely available, not just on long-distance routes such as Shikoku and Santiago but also on shorter and more local ones.

In 2007, I visited the Lourdes grotto at Cleator Moor, in Cumbria, England, to observe the Lancaster Catholic Diocese's annual pilgrimage there. Most people came by car (as did the Bishop) or coaches—the latter greeted by volunteers with wheelchairs for infirm pilgrims—but there was also a group of young pilgrims who arrived carrying banners and singing hymns, having spent three days walking from Lancaster. Regional and local Japanese pilgrimages I have studied, such as the eighty-eight-site Shikoku-replica pilgrimage around Shōdoshima in the Inland Sea, also have a similar mixture of walkers, pilgrims groups in microbuses (Shōdoshima's roads being too winding and narrow for coaches), and those using cars.

This diversity can cause tensions and complaints within the pilgrim community. Walkers in Shikoku have complained in their journals about bus pilgrims, especially when they feel a disjunction between the peace and quiet of the paths they have been on and the noise and chaos they encounter when arriving at temples full of hordes of pilgrims descending from buses. Those who have walked several hundred miles to Santiago do not always feel well disposed to those who arrive by plane or train, or when encountering pilgrims who travel by bicycle. Some consider walking to be the only true way to do the pilgrimage, airily describing anyone not on foot as 'inauthentic' and 'tourists', and making dismissive remarks about cyclists with expensive bicycles and special cycle clothes. Sometimes those using buses and cars seem to feel similarly: when my wife and I walked the Shikoku pilgrimage, several bus pilgrims commented that we were doing it the 'right way' and wished that they could be younger and so able to do so as well.

Not everyone is of that view. Priests in Shikoku sometimes have commented to me that those on foot are often more interested in hiking than devotion—arguing that those on buses spend much longer in prayer at the temples than walkers. Hence there are those who consider that the pilgrims who spend longer at the temples (such as those who travel by bus) are really the devout and authentic ones. A young man doing the Shikoku pilgrimage by car made the point clearly to us when we met him at one of the temples near the end of the route. Perhaps rather smugly we said that we had walked for over five weeks and were just a couple of days from completing the route. Rather than being impressed, he simply said that in the time it took us to walk it once he could do the pilgrimage six times, thus gaining far more merit than us walkers. In his view, it was the doing, not the way it was done or the time taken, that was critical, and he clearly felt that doing it more times made him more 'authentic' than someone just walking it once.

In reality, complaints or contrasts between walkers and others are unreasonable, as are notions of who is or is not an 'authentic' pilgrim. There are no specific texts that state that Muslims must make arduous overland journeys or that pilgrims in Shikoku or Santiago must walk in order to be 'authentic'. The image of 'two pilgrims together' in Shikoku does not discriminate between those on foot and other types of pilgrim; all are similarly travelling with Kōbō Daishi. Pilgrims walked in earlier times because there was little choice. As has been seen, the historical evidence shows that wherever new modes of travel and convenient ways to get to distant sites has developed, they have been eagerly embraced.

The medieval English pilgrims who used boats to speed their journeys to Santiago, or the modern Senegalese Muslims who fly in to Jeddah International airport to do the *hajj* rather than making a long and precarious overland journey across the Sahara, are not lesser or less authentic pilgrims because they have chosen such means of travel. They have expressed pragmatic attitudes towards their pilgrimages and have embraced modern means of transport because such things, along with modern health facilities and better accommodations, have made pilgrimage more accessible, reduced the threat of death along the way, and opened it up to more people across gender and age lines. The point was made aptly by a female pilgrim visiting the Lady of the Realm shrine in Vietnam when asked by researcher Philip Taylor if it was correct to make pilgrimages on air-conditioned buses and drink beer on the way. She answered, in effect, why shouldn't they make the journey as comfortable and enjoyable as possible? While she felt it would be wrong to drink beer at the shrine itself (that was a place for devotion), to do so elsewhere during the pilgrimage was fine.

The allure of transport

Transport itself can be an important part of the pilgrimage experience as well as a setting for ritual and devotional practices. Pilgrims travelling together in Shikoku commonly turn their buses into moving places of worship, with pilgrim guides leading them in prayer as they travel. In the early 20th century, Indian Railways, in a bid to persuade people unaccustomed to long-distance travel to use its services, specifically emphasized how useful trains could be in visiting distant pilgrimage sites, and developed links with religious organizations to this effect. Hindu authorities, recognizing that the railways could transform previously local shrines into national pilgrimage centres (as happened at Hardwar), affirmed that using trains was a legitimate means of doing pilgrimages. Buddhist organizations promoting pilgrimages to Indian sites such as Bodh Gaya did likewise and, like their Hindu counterparts, even talked about train travel as a form of austerity.

As such, railways rapidly became an accepted part of the pilgrimage process and experience in India, as they have elsewhere. Tibetan pilgrims were among those who were deeply impressed by the railways, many abandoning traditional practices of walking to Indian Buddhist sites in favour of going by rail. Many came to regard the rail journey as a highlight of their travels. Other modes of transport have similarly proved popular, increasing pilgrim numbers and becoming integrated into the wider sphere of pilgrim practices. In Shikoku, for example, from the 1930s onwards, cable cars started to be built up to some of the pilgrimage's most remote mountain temples, and they have now largely been integrated into pilgrimage tour itineraries as the preferred means of ascent to such temples.

'It's your pilgrimage'

> Remember that there are no rules, that it's *your* pilgrimage...

This is the advice offered on the website of the Confraternity of St James (a UK organization dedicated to supporting the Santiago pilgrimage) to would-be pilgrims to Santiago. It articulates how pilgrimage offers scope for personalized practice, not just in how pilgrims choose to travel, but in how they interpret their pilgrimages and what they seek from them. It offers them a way of taking control of their spiritual lives, of engaging in a personal search for meaning, and of making direct contact with sacred figures and places. Places that, in the minds of pilgrims, radiate spiritual power, and where gods and other sacred figures are believed to be especially approachable, enable them to experience that power directly, personally, and unmediated by religious authorities.

The notion of it being 'your pilgrimage' is evident in the multiplicity of motives and experiences pilgrims have. In talking to pilgrims in Japan over the years I have heard hundreds of stories about why they decided to become pilgrims or to do a particular route, and about their varying experiences. In short, for every pilgrim there is an individual story, motivation, and set of experiences. This is so even when pilgrims travel in organized groups or when they take part in pilgrimages which are preordained processes and rituals such as the *hajj* or the mountain ascent of Nhlangakazi by the Shembe Church pilgrims. Following a similar series of rituals to everyone else does not mean that pilgrims' reasons for taking part and experiences while doing so are all the same. Abdellah Hammoudi, discussing his pilgrimage to Mecca, was struck by the melting pot dimensions of the *hajj* but he also noted how the pilgrims he travelled with had different agendas from him, some, for example, devoting time to business and commerce as well as the *hajj* rituals during their visits. His experiences were personal and differed from fellow-pilgrims in the same party, as theirs clearly did from his.

A group of Shikoku pilgrims I travelled with by bus exemplified this individualized diversity. All wore standard pilgrimage clothing, participated in group rituals, were of similar ages, and came from similar social backgrounds in the same city. Yet talking to each individually, I found they all had their own reasons and motives for going, their own understandings of their journeys, and their own experiences, from the man intent on taking photographs (and with little interest in devotion) to a lady who prayed earnestly at each site as a memorial for her recently deceased husband. What they took away from their pilgrimages included a sense of togetherness as a group and of shared experience, as well as a personal set of experiences, motives, and meanings. They travelled in a group while doing their own pilgrimages.

While it is thus difficult to express all the reasons why people become pilgrims, studies of pilgrims in numerous settings have produced very similar results, showing that generally they express multiple reasons for so doing, and that a number of fairly common themes can be found cross-culturally. In some cases it may be the appeal of communal worship, of being together with and forming a bond with fellow-believers. This is clearly the case when Shembe church pilgrims ascend their sacred mountain together and thus feel a bond as well as a sense of unity with their founder, who initiated the mountain pilgrimage and whose steps they were retracing. Pilgrims who have done the *hajj*, such as Malcolm X, have expressed a similar feeling, as did the group of pilgrims from Tenrikyō, the Japanese new religion, with whom I made a pilgrimage to Tenri. Returning to a centre of one's religion or to sites associated with its holy figures provides an intensification, reaffirmation, and reinvigoration of faith. This is something that pilgrims who visit Shikoku in groups led by their Buddhist temple priest have emphasized to me. It is an emotion that may equally be felt by Catholic pilgrimage groups going with their priest or bishop to shrines such as Lourdes and supporting, as they do so, fellow-believers who are suffering and sick.

For the dead and the afterlife

The symbolic notion of pilgrimage as a metaphor for life and as a journey to enlightenment or spiritual transcendence may be significant for some pilgrims, although it is more common for them to express more pragmatic reasons for their journeys, linked either with making things better in this life or thereafter. Performing pilgrimages for the benefit of a deceased family member or for the benefit of family ancestors is frequently a major motivation. This is common in Hindu contexts, where pilgrims may carry the ashes of their departed to sacred rivers where the ashes will be immersed and the spirits thereby released from the bonds of this world.

It is also important for many Japanese pilgrims, seen widely, for example, in Shikoku and on the thirty-three-temple Saikoku pilgrimage, where many pilgrims say that they are doing such pilgrimages on behalf of their ancestors and deceased kin, in the belief that this aids their passage to the Buddhist Pure Land. They do it also for their own benefit. Shikoku legends are replete with stories of pilgrims being absolved of their bad karma through the pilgrimage, as was indicated by the story of Emon Saburō. The legendary origins of the Saikoku pilgrimage involve the lord of the underworld, Enma, showing a Buddhist monk the horrors that wrongdoers faced if they fell into the Buddhist hells at death, and then revealing to him how this could be avoided by performing a pilgrimage to thirty-three temples dedicated to Kannon. As a result, in Saikoku and Shikoku lore, doing these pilgrimages is seen as a means of eradicating sins, saving people from falling into the Buddhist hells, and allowing them to attain salvation. Beliefs that performing pilgrimages can wipe away transgressions in preparation for an afterlife are recurrent in Catholic contexts too, seen in the early penitential pilgrimages church courts ordered malefactors to do, and the indulgences and promises of remission of sins that church authorities have historically offered to encourage people to make pilgrimages.

Leaving your problems behind and seeking healing

Sometimes pilgrims are motivated by the wish to leave their personal problems behind by escaping from their ordinary existence and going on the road, where they may then confront their problems on their travels. Examples of such attitudes are found widely, from the 15th century Franciscan friar Paul Walther who, unable to meet the requirements of his order, went on a pilgrimage to the Holy Land to purify his body of sin, to modern examples such as a middle-aged man I met in Shikoku who told me he had left home after losing his job and getting into repeated rows with his wife. His aim, he said, was to find himself, resolve his problems, and then go home to ask his wife to forgive him and start anew.

Romantic problems can also play a role, as is demonstrated by the Shikoku pilgrimage made by Takamure Itsue in 1918 as she sought to deal with the grief of a disastrous love affair. Takamure wrote a series of articles for a regional newspaper, later turned into a book, about her pilgrimage experiences, which show how she drew strength from her travels, her fellow pilgrims, and from confronting the hardships she encountered in the world of pilgrimage. As she did so she resolved her problems, returned to marry the man in question, set up home with him in Tokyo, and in time became a widely respected literary figure and feminist historian. Her story continues to motivate young women in Japan, including some who have become pilgrims to follow in her footsteps. One day I was talking with the wife of a Shikoku temple priest when a solitary young female pilgrim walked into the temple courtyard. The priest's wife immediately commented that she had talked to several young women who were doing the Shikoku on foot alone in this way, and that they were frequently motivated by Takamure and doing it to get away from a failed love affair.

Along with the wish for emotional healing are hopes for physical cures. These have abounded among pilgrims historically, playing a major role in eras when people had little possibility of medical cures for illness. They remain potent even in the present era and in cultures that benefit from advanced medical aid. The rows of pilgrims in wheelchairs being assisted to take the waters at Lourdes are just one such example, as are the petitions for healing and good health made by pilgrims in Japan, and the supplications of those who visit the shrine at Tinos, many of whom seek alleviation of illness and physical suffering.

In New Mexico, USA, the shrine of El Santuario de Chimayo receives a regular flow of Hispanic Catholic and Native American pilgrims, sometimes on crutches or in wheelchairs, who believe that the shrine possesses special curative properties. The shrine, built on ground believed to be sacred in Native American traditional religion, refers on its website to its reputation for and history of miracle cures and it provides numerous pilgrim testimonials about the healing of all manner of problems ranging from cancers and infertility to the emotional pains. Gratitude for having a wish granted also spurs many to make repeat pilgrimages there to offer thanks, a theme found repeatedly across the pilgrimage spectrum. Others leave behind items such as crutches that they claim are no longer needed after they have visited the shrine.

Vows and pilgrims

Sometimes people make pilgrimages as a result of a vow after, for example, calling on a saint's help in a time of crisis and pledging to do a pilgrimage if their prayers are heard. The pilgrims crawling up the steps at Tinos, for example, may be motivated by vows they have made and the need to show their sincerity to the deity in order to attain her grace. It was not uncommon in medieval Christian contexts for people to make such vows, and studies of Santiago pilgrims have shown that they also may, to this day, set out on pilgrimage as a result of calling on St James's help and vowing to make a pilgrimage to his holy place if their prayers are answered.

Murukan, the deity at Kataragama in Sri Lanka, has a reputation for helping those in need who call for his help, for intervening when other deities do not, for responding to the requests of those who vow to make pilgrimages to his shrine if he does intercede, and for being pleased with acts of self-mortification that express the pilgrim's devotion. As such, the severe austerities endured by those who make pilgrimages to Kataragama are often because of the vows they have made to Murukan in order to gain his grace at a time of predicament and crisis. One man depicted in a 1966 *National Geographic* article about Katagarama, for example, had vowed to make the pilgrimage each year if his father (wrongly accused of murder) was found innocent. He *was* exonerated, and so his son returned each year on pilgrimage to Kataragama to perform austerities and thank Murukan.

In Japan, too, one encounters similar stories of desperation and vows. One man I interviewed, for example, ran a pilgrimage association in his home town and spent a lot of his time supporting Shikoku pilgrimage activities. He told me that he had been called up, unwillingly, into the Japanese armed forces in World War Two and, in despair on the frontline in China as comrades fell around him, he called on Kōbō Daishi to save him, vowing to go on the Shikoku pilgrimage if he survived. He did survive, and as a result, after Japan's surrender, he went to Shikoku in 1946, walked the pilgrimage, and thereafter devoted much effort to encouraging others to become Daishi followers and pilgrims.

Worldly needs and requests

Worldly assistance in all manner of daily life concerns—from success in a child's education to family welfare, marital harmony, safe childbearing, economic well-being, and business prosperity—are common pilgrim requests and major motivations for their travels. Studies of pilgrim requests in Japan have shown how all of these concerns feature widely in the prayers pilgrims make and the prayer request slips they leave at temples. The votive tablets and petitions left by pilgrims at Christian shrines such as Walsingham also testify to the ubiquity of such worldly requests; reading what pilgrims had sought there and at other shrines in Europe reminded me very much, in different languages, of what I have read when studying pilgrim petitions in Japan.

The Rajasthani pilgrims studied by Ann Gold made frequent local pilgrimages to seek similar boons from their gods. Likewise, Philip Taylor's account of Vietnamese pilgrims visiting the shrine of the Lady of the Realm shows that pilgrims who belong to Vietnam's emergent small business and market-trader classes are particularly keen on praying for commercial and business success. Pilgrims rarely limit themselves to just one request, and frequently seek multiple benefits on their travels—again something I have come across in diverse shrines in different countries. Shrine authorities at times consider such excessive petitioning to be inappropriate. Priests in Japan have at times commented on the tendency of some pilgrims to ask for a multiplicity of benefits, while a handwritten sign I saw in 2004 by the box where pilgrims left their requests at Walsingham summed this point up clearly (see Figure 10). It said simply, in capitals:

NO MORE THAN THREE PETITIONS PER PILGRIM PER PILGRIMAGE, PLEASE.

10. **Walsingham: admonition for pilgrims.**

Worries and mortality

Accounts, whether of those on foot or travelling by more speedy means of transport, indicate that no matter how one travels, a mixture of stress, turmoil, and exhilaration are likely to be parts of the pilgrimage experience. Foot pilgrims focus particularly on the physical toil of pilgrimage, with blisters, rain, and worries about where to find toilets and where to stay overnight being a recurrent theme in Shikoku pilgrim diaries and accounts. Although on one level pilgrimage may involve leaving behind the normal structures and issues that shape lives—such as the need to adhere to fixed schedules of work and so on—few pilgrims become wholly detached in such respects. Whether they are travelling on foot, by bus, or by other means, concerns about time and schedules (especially when there is a return flight to catch) remain a continuing issue for many, as do such day-to-day concerns as getting to a lodging or finding somewhere to sleep before it is too late.

Mortality is another theme that surfaces regularly in pilgrim accounts. Even in an age when few pilgrims actually face the dangers and possibilities of death that were commonplace in earlier eras, doing a pilgrimage, notably when walking long distances, can remind pilgrims of their own mortality—a theme identified by Nancy Frey in her study of the stories and experiences of late-20th century Santiago walkers. Such views also surface in Shikoku pilgrim accounts. This is not just in the recurrent sense that a pilgrimage may be a turning point in one's life, with notions of the pilgrim dying to their earlier lives and seeing, or hoping, through their pilgrimages to return renewed, and spiritually and emotionally reborn. It is also often tinged with a sense of how they are travelling paths trodden by earlier generations, something that can be emphasized by the markers along pilgrim trails memorializing pilgrims who died there in previous eras, and by memories of previous, and now departed, family members who had made similar pilgrimages in past times.

What now?

A further issue that recurs in pilgrim narratives across cultures, especially as people come to the end of their journeys, can be expressed by the simple question: what now? On one level a pilgrimage may end when the pilgrim has reached a specific goal or final destination, or has returned home. Yet for many pilgrims the end-point may also be (at least in the ideal scenario) a starting point for the rest of their lives, from which they set out with a determination to start anew and to let what they have learned on pilgrimage guide them henceforth.

The image of pilgrimage as a means of self-discovery and transformation runs through pilgrim accounts and in the resolutions many make (not always successfully) that on returning home their lives will be changed and old habits discarded. Felix Fabri, a German pilgrim to the Christian Holy Land in the 15th century, considered he had returned transformed to start life anew. Indeed, such was the strength of this feeling that he noted that even his hometown of Ulm looked different as a result. Malcolm X, the American Muslim who went to Mecca with an avowedly hostile attitude to whites and non-Muslims, returned home a changed man determined to preach to and work for people of all ethnicities.

When Kagita Chūsaburō, a middle-aged Japanese businessman, became ill due to overwork in 1961, he chose to walk the Shikoku pilgrimage to get well again. As he did so, he realized that he needed to reform his entire life, and by the time he returned home he had determined to start anew in more socially useful ways. His new path included giving up business to engage in local politics, serving as mayor of his local town and striving, in the best way he felt possible, for the benefit of his surrounding community. Such resolve is typical of the emotions that surface as pilgrims come to the end of their immediate physical journeys and begin to reflect on their meanings. Pilgrimage thus can serve as a catalyst for

changing lives and intentions—even if for many such determination
can wane once they have got home.

Repetition and addiction

One of the most recurrent pilgrim reactions to the 'what now'
question is to think about going again, either repeating the same
pilgrimage or going elsewhere. Pilgrimage is not a 'once-in-a-
lifetime' event, and it is certainly true of contemporary pilgrimage
that there are many who do go on pilgrimages again and again.
This is in contrast to earlier eras, when the threat of death en
route was much higher and when transport was less rapid,
meaning long distances were not so easily managed. In such
times it was more common for trips to distant places, on often
dangerous routes—such as Mecca, Shikoku, or Santiago—to be
done just once in a lifetime.

Yet even in past eras there were those who sought to return to
distant places or to incorporate numerous local pilgrimages into
their array of pilgrimage experiences, and to become incessant
pilgrims. The Norfolk female mystic Margery Kempe, for example,
made numerous pilgrimages in the 15th century, visiting the
Christian Holy Land, Santiago de Compostela, and several other
pilgrimage sites on the continent such as Rome and Assisi, as well
as many sites within England. Kempe collected indulgences from
the sites she visited, relied on alms and begging to sustain her, and
frequently annoyed her fellow pilgrims by excessive demonstrations
of piety and recurrent weeping. Each pilgrimage she went on
seemed to increase her resolve and desire to go on another, as her
life became a cycle of pilgrimage activities.

Records from Shikoku from the 17th century onwards show a
number of pilgrims who made numerous journeys around the
island, from the ascetic Shinnen, who published the first pilgrimage
guidebooks and collection of miracle tales, who did the pilgrimage
some twenty times, and who died there in 1691, to Tada Emon, who

died in 1862 having done the pilgrimage 136 times. Most famous of all is Nakatsuka Mōhei, who went to Shikoku to walk the pilgrimage in 1865 to get over his unhappiness when his parents refused to allow him to marry a local girl. Nakatsuka, at the end of his first circuit of pilgrimage route, just carried on, eventually doing the pilgrimage 282 times, living 'on the road' for most of the subsequent fifty-seven years, until, in 1922, he died—still on the route.

Today, examples of those who do repeated pilgrimages are widespread, not least because such journeys can be made more easily and quickly, and because economic circumstances allow more people the means to do so. While perhaps few are as eclectic in their travels as the Japanese couple who made numerous pilgrimages to Buddhist sites in Japan, China, and India and then visited European Christian sites, there are many examples across traditions and countries of people who repeatedly perform pilgrimages. All the pilgrims on one organized bus tour I travelled with in Shikoku spent the return journey discussing which pilgrimages they wanted to try next, and officials who run pilgrimage tours in Japan have frequently commented to me that many of their customers are repeaters who travel again and again, either to Shikoku or to other sites of pilgrimage in Japan.

I have interviewed many Shikoku pilgrims who spend long periods of their life on pilgrimage while others spend their whole lives on the pilgrimage path. One such man had done the Shikoku route 110 times, sometimes on foot but in later years by bus, as a pilgrimage guide and group leader. In his eighties he was spending sixty days a year on the pilgrimage trail, leading bus party groups and devoting the time between journeys to preparing for the next pilgrimage and taking part in related promotional events. Such repeated performances can advance one's social status within the pilgrimage community. The Shikoku pilgrimage temples award the title *sendatsu* (pilgrimage guide) to pilgrims who have done the pilgrimage four or more times; by the early 2000s some 12,000 people held that title. Many join pilgrimage associations, receive the monthly newsletter sent by the pilgrimage temples to all registered *sendatsu*, and join in various pilgrimage publicity and devotional activities. Such repeated performances have been likened to an addiction by priests and pilgrims alike, with the phrase *Shikokubyō* ('Shikoku illness') widely used in the pilgrimage community to describe this 'addiction'.

When I was at Knock in Ireland I overheard groups of pilgrims discussing which other sites they had been to or wanted to visit next. Marian shrines such as Lourdes, along with that of Padre Pio, the Capuchin friar whose claims of stigmata gave rise to a powerful pilgrimage cult at San Giovanni Rotondo in Italy from the early 20th century onwards, featured repeatedly in their conversations. Well-off Muslims may do the *hajj* annually, while Simon Coleman's studies of pilgrims at Walsingham show that some visit it so regularly that it becomes their 'second home'. Philip Taylor's study of Vietnamese pilgrimages indicates that many pilgrims visit the shrine of the Lady of the Realm repeatedly and that many of them (particularly women) travel round the country to a number of sites on a regular basis, in a round of pilgrimages that fits into, rather than being set apart from, their everyday lives.

Those who visit Santiago de Compostela may similarly find it addictive and are drawn back to doing it again or to volunteering as helpers in pilgrim hostels along the route. Many join regional or national societies such as the Confraternity of St James to continue their association with the pilgrimage and make it a lifelong activity. Sometimes people visit places as pilgrims and then, reluctant to leave, stay on afterwards in order to be permanently in the site of their pilgrimage devotions. Such phenomena have been noted by scholars at numerous sites around the world, ranging from pilgrims who have taken up residence at San Giovanni Rotondo in Italy to be forever in the place of Padre Pio to the Hindu devotees called Kashivasi, who come as pilgrims to the Indian sacred city of Varanasi (known also in Hindu contexts as Kashi, 'City of Light') and then stay on permanently.

Such examples show that pilgrimage is neither separate from the normal lives of participants nor transitory in nature. The recurrence with which people perform pilgrimages, sometimes becoming permanent pilgrims on the road, treating pilgrimage places as second homes to return to again and again, or becoming residents of sites they have journeyed to, shows that pilgrimage need not be an exceptional activity that happens rarely or perhaps just once in a lifetime. While it can be about being restless and wanting to get away from normal daily existences to find things anew, it also is closely associated with reinforcing the everyday nature of existence. Similarly, while it involves going away from home to places where something spiritually potent and empowering may be encountered, it also is associated with thoughts about home—something that will be seen further when we look at the importance of souvenirs, shopping, and entertainment in pilgrimage contexts.

Chapter 5
Festivity, tourism, and souvenirs

Every year, on 26 January, members of the Japanese religion Tenrikyō engage in a mass pilgrimage to honour their founder Nakayama Miki. In 1986 on the 100th anniversary of Nakayama's passing I was invited to take part in this pilgrimage by members of a local Tenrikyō church in the city of Kobe, where I then lived. Around one hundred people boarded coaches there for the two-hour journey to Tenri, during which Tenrikyō members chatted to me about my research and the day ahead; they also engaged in prayers and recitations of Tenrikyō liturgy led by senior church members. Arriving at Tenri, the group joined a massive throng of pilgrims who visited the main shrine, offered prayers, engaged in various rituals, and attended a huge communal service overseen by the movement's leader. We then had lunch and interacted socially with groups from other Tenrikyō branches.

Later on the pilgrims attended special lectures on Tenrikyō faith, visited Tenrikyō institutions in the town, and browsed the various shops selling Tenrikyō ritual implements, clothing, texts, and souvenirs. In the early evening we reconvened at a pre-arranged time for the return journey and, as we boarded the coach, each adult was handed a can of cold beer specially produced by a major Japanese brewery and embossed with special Tenrikyō 100th anniversary commemoration insignia. As the bus drew away we happily imbibed the beer, chatted sociably, and relaxed.

Celebration and pilgrimage

This picture reflects a pattern widely noted in studies of pilgrimage, of how people commonly behave in a more austere manner, focused on prayer and solemn behaviour, perhaps also eschewing things such as alcohol, on the way to and during their pilgrimages, while return journeys are seen as times for relaxation and celebration. On a bus pilgrimage in Shikoku our guide told us we should not drink alcohol at lunchtime, since we had other temples to visit in the afternoon. In the evening, however, once we had reached our lodgings, he had no problem if anyone wanted a beer, and after we had visited the last temple and completed the pilgrimage, he insisted we had a celebratory meal accompanied by beer even though it was still the middle of the day. The communal feast at the end of the *hajj* can be seen in this light as well, as an example of celebration at the culmination of a pilgrimage.

Relaxation, celebration, and entertainment are often woven into pilgrimage structures, with pilgrims who may have been abstemious while on pilgrimage subsequently 'letting off steam' at the end of their journeys or on the way home. Unsurprisingly there are plentiful places around pilgrimage sites to cater for (and encourage) such inclinations. They are evidence also of the commercial acumen of those who live around pilgrimage sites and who view pilgrims primarily as a source of economic support. The entertainment quarters that grew around the Japanese shrines of Ise from the 17th century onwards are but one example of this.

Celebrations and festivities are, for many pilgrims, an integral part of their pilgrimages, and the scope pilgrimages offer for play, sightseeing, and shopping, as well as for prayer, devotion, and ascetic activities, has been influential in their appeal. This does at times cause tension and unease; the Catholic Church's concerns about some of the entrepreneurial activities that surround Lourdes is one such example, while complaints about frivolous behaviour are frequently made by religious officials as well as by (and about) pilgrims at many sites.

Nonetheless, for the most part pilgrims have been less than hostile to the commercial dimensions of pilgrimage, and show this not only by readily embracing new modes of travel and new comforts, but by welcoming the availability at pilgrimage sites of festivities, entertainment facilities, and material goods such as souvenirs to take home. Religious authorities, too, have generally not just accepted such activities as a natural and necessary concomitant of drawing large numbers of people to their sites, but have frequently been deeply instrumental in promoting them and at times also providing theological legitimations for such activities.

Creating entertainment, attracting pilgrims

A good example can be seen in Sarah Thal's study of Konpira Shrine, a famed Shinto pilgrimage centre in Shikoku, Japan, which shows the various ways in which shrine priests strove to ensure a steady flow of pilgrims to their site between the 16th and early 20th centuries. The shrine, atop a mountain above the town of Kotohira in the plains of northern Shikoku, has long been a centre for religious devotion and pilgrimage, with its deities having a reputation for providing all manner of efficacious benefits.

Its priests were conscious, however, that as travel opportunities increased from the 17th century on, and as people became aware of other pilgrimage sites whose deities also offered spiritual rewards, Konpira faced increasing competition. They could not simply rely on the shrine's reputation; to maintain a constant flow of pilgrims they had to develop and amend its appeal in accord with changing market patterns and pilgrim interests. To keep abreast of such aspects they travelled around the country checking what other shrines were doing and working out what new trends could be incorporated at Konpira. Priests of my current acquaintance at Japanese pilgrimage centres similarly keep an eye on what other sites are doing.

Consequently, Konpira's priests continually added to their shrine by incorporating fresh attractions such as new deities, practices, and worldly benefits. They created new places for pilgrims to worship, opening up additional paths up the mountain to improve the flow of pilgrims, increasing the number of wayside shrines pilgrims would pass by and be tempted to leave donations at. They also organized entertainment events, including festivals, theatrical displays, and Sumo tournaments to further enhance the appeal of the town and shrine. If they felt uneasy about some of the entertainments that occurred (just as at Ise, prostitution and gambling proved to be particularly strong attractions) they nonetheless considered that having a bustling town and thriving shrine were more attractive—and would thus please the shrine gods—than stamping out such activities, causing the flow of pilgrims to dry up and the gods to become unhappy.

Festivity and spectacle have repeatedly provided alluring contributions to the growth and attractiveness of pilgrimage sites. They were a recurrent feature of Chinese pilgrimage in earlier times. In the 17th century, for example, the Chinese writer Zhang Dai was especially impressed by the hawkers, hubbub, and festivity when he visited the mountain pilgrimage site of Tai Shan. Miao-feng Shan, a sacred mountain some thirty miles from Beijing on which stands a temple enshrining the compassionate female deity Pi-hsia Yuan-chun, developed as a popular pilgrimage centre in which entertainment and piety sat side by side. Records show that by the 18th century facilities such as rest houses served the needs of the pilgrim community, and that by the mid-19th century shrine representatives sought to increase pilgrim numbers by posting advertisements about the pilgrimage in Beijing.

Entertainment played a role too, with pilgrims being drawn by jugglers, tightrope walkers, and folk-opera troupes at the site.

Improved transportation, including a railroad from Beijing built in 1896, also enhanced Miao-feng Shan's popularity, as did guidebooks produced by the companies running the railway that promoted the festivities there. Austere practices continued also to be part of the pilgrimage for those who so wanted; documentary film evidence from the 1920s shows how, along with processions, music, and dances, some pilgrims dressed as penitents and prostrated themselves repeatedly as they ascended the mountain.

Pilgrimages came to a virtual halt during the turbulent period of warfare from the 1930s onwards, while later the hostility of China's Maoist regime to religion continued to restrict the practice. In more recent times, as China has opened up to tourists and become more relaxed in its attitudes towards traditional religious practices, the mountain has again become a pilgrimage and tourist centre. Nowadays, Miao-feng Shan is advertised online as an area where one can walk along hiking trails in the footsteps of pilgrims of yore, and as a site where pilgrims can pray for various benefits.

Philip Taylor's description of the annual autumn festival at the Lady of the Realm shrine in Vietnam provides a vibrant contemporary example of how festivity and pilgrimage interact. Pilgrim numbers peak at this time as people flock to offer prayers, take part in rituals, consult mediums, and have fun. They watch dance performances by transvestite troupes, listen to operatic concerts, wander through a huge fairground with booths, rides, and games, eat at food stalls, enjoy cafes and bars with karaoke machines, and shop at markets with innumerable stalls. They also pray and make offerings, for prayer and play form part of the whole experience of the site rather than being distinctly separate activities.

Holidays, holy days, and markets

This interweaving of festivity and pilgrimage is neither specifically modern nor culturally specific. While the examples I have just cited are from Asia, similar patterns and linkages are found elsewhere. In medieval England (as in Europe in general) pilgrims flocked to shrines on saints' feast days, which were the times when saints were believed to be most open to petitions. They were also occasions when markets would be held at or around cathedrals and churches. Commercial interests, markets, and pilgrimage activities thus intersected each other, while feast days were for many in the medieval world the only time off they had from their labours. These holy days provided the etymological derivation of the word we now use for such festivity and time off: 'holidays'.

This correlation of festivities, holy days, holidays, pilgrimage, and markets is also reflected linguistically in Japan, where the word for special days when deities and Buddhist figures of worship are specially approachable—their holy days—is *ennichi* ('day of good karmic connections'). *Ennichi* also means 'market' and the two meanings were, like holy days and holidays, largely synonymous. Temples would hold special prayer days that attracted crowds of pilgrims (often drawn by the temporary opening to the public view of normally hidden sacred icons), while market stalls would be set up so that pilgrims could buy souvenirs and engage in commercial activities and prayer. Stall holders and merchants, likewise, could engage in their commerce and have the opportunity to pray and seek boons from the gods as well.

Relics and souvenirs

The associations of festivity, pilgrimage, and markets are manifest also in an area that probably the large majority of pilgrims engage in: shopping for things to take home as mementos and reminders of the sites they visit. It is a rare pilgrimage centre that does not offer plentiful opportunities to acquire lucky charms, amulets, statuettes, relics, and other items, or that is not surrounded by shops and stalls selling souvenirs, often with religious themes, to take home

11. Religious trinkets and souvenirs on sale outside the Catholic pilgrimage shrine at Einseideln in Switzerland.

(see Figure 11). The oft-criticized kitsch and commercialism of Lourdes, and the commingling of commerce and piety at Mecca and Medina are reflective of a common pattern in this respect.

The early Christian pilgrims who visited Jerusalem brought back items ranging from splinters of the 'True Cross' to vials of holy water from the River Jordan, thereby enabling them to have something of the Holy Land in their homes on their return. Medieval Christian pilgrims assiduously acquired, from the sites they visited, pilgrim badges that signified the protection of the saints they had visited, and that served as mementos of their visits and as signs of their status as pilgrims. Such badges were also advertising devices for their shrines, for which the production and marketing of pilgrim badges was a major commercial undertaking and an important source of income.

Water has long been a popular item to be brought back from pilgrimage sites. Just as the early Christian pilgrims brought back water from the River Jordan, so may Hindu pilgrims to Hardwar or Varanasi bring back small bottles of Ganges' water; and those visiting Hindu pilgrimage sites on other rivers often do the same. From Mecca, Muslim pilgrims may bring back a vial of water from the Zamzam well, while pilgrims to Catholic sites such as Lourdes and Knock, whose waters are claimed to have healing properties, may purchase special bottles (often with the inscription 'Holy Water: I prayed for you at Knock/Lourdes') in which to take shrine water home with them.

Other items found widely include statues and depictions of sacred figures, candles, amulets, items designated by shrines as relics, and medallions depicting the figures of worship at the shrine concerned. Many of these items are sold by the shrines themselves at their shops, and are used to enhance their pilgrimage cults, as with the tongue relics of St Anthony at Padua. Another Catholic example is from the Chapel of Our Lady of the Miraculous Medal in Paris, whose origins as a pilgrimage site date to an 1830 visitation by Mary seen by the Catholic novice Catherine Labouré. Mary told Catherine to make a medal (the 'Miraculous Medal') depicting Mary, which would bring benefits to its wearers. The shrine began to produce such medals, which rapidly became associated with all manner of miracles. Papal ratification of the apparitions further enhanced the site's status, as did claims that Mary appeared at her shrine at Einsiedeln in Switzerland holding a copy of the medal in 1835 and that Bernadette was wearing a Miraculous Medal when visited by Mary (apparently looking just as she did on the medal) at Lourdes in 1858. As a result, the shrine's medals have been in high demand, and pilgrims can purchase them at the shrine in various shapes, sizes, and quantities for their own use and to pass on to others.

Japanese pilgrimage sites usually sell a large variety of amulets associated with warding off bad luck and beckoning good fortune, as well as various religious regalia such as candles, incense, rosaries, Buddhist stoles, and (a fairly common item these days) key chains depicting sacred figures such as Kōbō Daishi. The Shri Mata Vaishno Devi shrine advertises on its website that pilgrims can buy a variety of items at the official shrine souvenir shops (including bags and laminated photos of the shrine's inner sanctum) unavailable elsewhere.

Pilgrimage shrines may have a monopoly on some items, such as amulets and the like that are blessed in religious services. This does not preclude vendors outside the shrines from offering pilgrims the opportunity to acquire a whole array of objects, often quite similar to those sold at the shrines, as reminders of their visits. Candles, rosaries, and statuettes are common at Japanese Buddhist as they are at European Catholic sites. At Mecca and Medina pilgrims can purchase numerous items such as prayer mats and consumer items including gold jewellery and Meccan wristwatches (often in gold or platinum). The streets around the cathedral at Santiago de Compostela have plentiful shops selling lucky charms, plaques, badges, pilgrims' walking sticks, numerous objects embossed with the name 'Santiago de Compostela', and badges and figurines of Xubi, the cheerful mascot of the 2010 Holy Year pilgrimage. The Pastilles de Lourdes with their reputed healing properties and statuettes of Mary at Lourdes, the arrays of Virgin Mary water bottles and snow shakers sold at Knock, and the key rings and various items depicting Buddhist figures found around pilgrimage sites in Japan, are other examples of the types of items available for purchase. Among the various items I have picked up at places of pilgrimage that I have visited, perhaps my favourite is a Kōbō Daishi pottery bottle that, when originally acquired outside one of the pilgrimage temples, contained Shikoku-brewed saké.

Schedules and shopping

The marketplace dynamics surrounding shrines and the opportunities for shopping contained therein are widely catered for in pilgrimage schedules; Hammoudi's *hajj* account shows how its schedule provided time for such activities. Studies of pilgrim behaviour at Lourdes, too, indicate how buying souvenirs and religious items forms an intrinsic element in pilgrim activities there. Bus tour schedules in Shikoku regularly include enough time for pilgrims to go to temple offices and get incense, amulets, and the like, and visit the souvenir shops at the temple gates; they also frequently include stops at popular tourist spots for further shopping.

Such is the demand for items to take home that those running shrines and temples, and merchants reliant on the pilgrimage trade in souvenirs, find themselves, as various stall-keepers and priests in Japan have said to me, under pressure to satisfy pilgrim wishes. Many people make repeated pilgrimages and want new items to take home each time as reminders of that specific pilgrimage. As a result, merchants along the route feel a constant need to produce new items to this end, and to ensure that they can continue to cater to (and encourage) pilgrims' desire to take home mementos.

Talismans, scrolls, and meanings

The acquisition of charms and souvenirs serves as a means of showing others that one has made a particular pilgrimage. Japanese pilgrims who went to Ise in earlier ages were frequently given alms by their fellow villagers to help them on their way. They were also expected, in return, to bring back Ise shrine amulets for the local shrine, thereby bringing the Ise deities back to the village to protect the community and, hopefully, guarantee a good harvest.

Pilgrims in Japan generally carry with them a pilgrim's book or scroll that is stamped at each pilgrimage temple they visit (see Figure 12). In earlier ages the pilgrim's book and stamps served as proof that the person had visited the pilgrimage sites she/he had acquired travel permits for. As such, it was essentially a legal

12. Pilgrim's book from Shikoku, inscribed with stamps and calligraphy of the temples visited.

document, but over time it became transformed into a spiritual item in the eyes of pilgrims, based on the belief that doing a pilgrimage such as Shikoku or Saikoku would eradicate one's bad karma. A completed pilgrimage book thus came to be seen as a passport to the Pure Land, and it became customary for such books to be placed in the coffins of deceased pilgrims for this reason. Santiago pilgrims who have walked at least 100 kilometres (or cyclists who have done 200) also acquire a similar 'passport'. Prior to departure they can acquire a *credencial* or pilgrim's record, which they get stamped at official sites along the way. On showing it at the cathedral in Santiago they may be issued with a Compostela, a Latin-inscribed certificate, signifying completion of the pilgrimage.

Items brought back from a pilgrimage are important as reminders of the place visited, of one's journey there, and as symbols of its power. Having an item—whether a statuette of Mary from Knock, a laminated photograph of the inner sanctum of Shri Mata

Vaishno Devi, a prayer mat from Mecca, or a souvenir badge of Xubi from Santiago—not only creates a link between the sacred place and home but also incorporates the spirit of the former in the latter as a continuing presence. It means the pilgrimage place is no longer distant, but continually present.

Studies of Santiago pilgrims indicate that they frequently take home numerous items from their pilgrimage, which then adorn their houses, such as the pilgrim's walking stick, the scallop shell symbol of St James, and the Compostela, which is often framed and hung up on display. Japanese pilgrims, too, may decorate their homes with ornate pilgrimage scrolls, which have for many pilgrims replaced the pilgrim's book as a key item to acquire. On starting pilgrimages such as Shikoku or Saikoku they can purchase a silken scroll, usually inscribed with Kōbō Daishi or Kannon at its centre, which is stamped with the temple insignia and ink-brush calligraphy at each temple. Once completed, the scroll is embossed and mounted on a brocade background, making it into a striking aesthetic object that is decorative while symbolically serving, because it has been stamped at each temple, as a miniature version of the pilgrimage itself. The scroll is a costly item; to purchase the basic silken scroll and pay for stamps at each temple and for the final embossing process can cost the equivalent of several hundred British pounds. It has become very popular among contemporary pilgrims, however, both as a status symbol and as an ornament hung up in the home as a sign and reminder of the pilgrimage. Indeed, several people have told me that they did certain pilgrimages in Japan because they wanted to get a particular scroll for their house, with the scroll thus becoming a motive for their pilgrimage.

Home, family, friendship, and love

In linking home and shrines, souvenirs and other items thus indicate that pilgrimage is not just about travel and going away but also about return and reaffirmations of home. They also serve as a means of emphasizing family and friendship ties. Bringing back things acquired at a distant shrine is a way of telling a friend or family member, who was unable to travel, that the pilgrim was thinking about them while at the shrine, so that they were 'there' in spirit.

Indeed, what to buy and for whom may form an important part of the pilgrimage shopping experience. During visits to various pilgrimage sites in Japan I have had conversations with pilgrims who were discussing what item might be good to bring back for a particular friend or relative. An elderly pilgrim couple at a Shikoku temple, for example, told me that they were looking for interesting lucky charms and souvenirs to take home to their grandchildren in the hope that the charms would bring them good fortune and that the souvenirs would entertain them.

In a souvenir shop in Knock full of rosaries, candles, bottles for holy water, and statuettes, I was fascinated by the conversation of two women who were commenting to each other about how a particular statuette would be just right for a particular cousin. In such ways pilgrims can share their pilgrimages with those back home. A plastic bottle bearing the inscription 'Holy Water: I prayed for you at Knock' is not simply a physical reminder and symbol of the spiritual power of the shrine, it is also a demonstration and message of the pilgrim's feelings for those she or he cares for back home, and a way of binding them closer together.

Money and aesthetics

The significance and meanings inherent in such items transcend the monetary, and, in the eyes of many beholders, also the aesthetic, value of the items acquired. As such, criticisms levelled at pilgrimage sites and pilgrims that the goods on sale there and the items pilgrims acquire are frequently tacky, cheap, and garish completely miss the point. Their significance is not in aesthetics but in the meanings they have for pilgrims and those at home alike, and in the fact that they contain and represent the spiritual presence and essence of the site or deities visited.

The vials that early Christian pilgrims acquired to bring back their River Jordan holy water were generally cheap not because pilgrims had no taste or because many of them were financially constrained, but because it was what they contained and what that signified, rather than the aesthetic value of the container, that was important. Similarly, a plastic Virgin Mary water bottle from Lourdes or Knock might look cheap and kitsch-like to some, but to those who see it as a means of bringing home something of Lourdes, of expressing the experience of having been there, and of manifesting feelings for loved ones, it has emotional value and qualities that transcend any questions of aesthetics.

Cost and aesthetics are unimportant when compared with symbolism and emotional meanings. Nonetheless, and this is something that becomes more significant as pilgrims become better-off, some pilgrimage items may be revered and sought out for their aesthetic qualities as well. Cheap goods, pilgrim badges, water containers, and the like might have been standard for most pilgrims but the well-off have rarely shied away from purchasing more expensive items when they could, such as gold watches and costly prayer rugs from Mecca, or the expensive and beautiful scrolls acquired by Japanese pilgrims. They demonstrate not only that pilgrims continue to place great store by what they can purchase and bring back from their travels, but that as they have more money they are likely to spend more and seek out more expensive items.

Overall, then, the thriving souvenir markets of pilgrimage sites, and the goods that are brought home from them, can be seen to be important elements in pilgrimage, full of deep meaning for pilgrims and their families, and not just some unsightly intrusion on the sacred nature of the practice. They further emphasize how play, commerce, consumerism, tourism, and entertainment are in no way disjunctions from the essence of pilgrimage, but rather that they are critical elements of its very fabric.

Seeing sites along the way

Along with the shrines and such places that are the main focus of their travels, pilgrims may want to visit sightseeing places along the way with no religious significance, as diversions or codas to their journeys. Medieval Venetian Holy Land package tours, for example, were frequently structured to accommodate such desires, and, after the serious business of veneration involved in visiting sacred sites in Jerusalem and so on, they would take pilgrims on to Egypt to view historic sites there.

By the 19th century tourist sites and attractions close to Japan's Saikoku pilgrimage route became a regular feature of pilgrim guidebooks; hot spring resorts, always popular in Japan, were a particular attraction to pilgrims keen to relax during their pilgrimages or on their way home. Contemporary pilgrimage tour operators in Shikoku report that many who come to the island on pilgrimage want also to see other famous tourist sites there as they do so. Two spectacular gorges in the centre of the island, Ritsurin Park in Takamatsu, northern Shikoku, one of the country's most famous Japanese gardens, the Konpira shrine, and the Dogo hot spring resort are all particularly popular attractions in Shikoku, and are included in many pilgrimage itineraries. Nowadays, too, places with esteemed local cuisine also prove popular diversions, so that the opportunity to enjoy the gastronomic delights of the island has become a prominent feature of pilgrimage tour advertisements.

The pilgrims who visit Tinos to perform their penitential acts and who stay on to have a holiday, swim, and shop are similarly showing that they view pilgrimage not as a hermetically sealed activity separate from pleasure, but as intertwined with (and in many respects thus inseparable from) tourism. The Rajasthani pilgrims Ann Gold describes on their Indian bus pilgrimage visited sacred sites and immersed the ashes of their deceased kin in the river at the Hindu holy city Gaya, but they also took advantage of opportunities for relaxation. For many, indeed, the highlight of their journey was not at the sacred Hindu sites where they performed their rituals, but at the beach when they bathed in the Bay of Bengal.

Including a variety of places such as museums, beaches, and the like in one's pilgrimage travels is common in India, especially for those who may not have the finances to travel frequently and for whom seeing other parts of the country's cultural and scenic heritage may be readily incorporated into pilgrimage tours. Pilgrimage is very much at the heart of domestic Indian tourism, and many of India's main pilgrimage sites such as Hardwar, Pushkar, and Varanasi are simultaneously tourist destinations. India's growing middle classes have shown a particular keenness to travel and see the cultural richness of their country, while at the same time projecting themselves, even as they visit (and pray at) places such as Hardwar and Pushkar, primarily as tourists. At such places, along with their temples and places of prayer, a variety of tourist-oriented attractions have also developed including, at Hardwar, amusement and theme parks.

Similarly, many of Christianity's major pilgrimage sites, such as Rome and Jerusalem, whose historic and cultural significance and resources offer plentiful scope for combining pilgrimage and sightseeing, have long been tourist magnets. People who visit Rome as pilgrims, besides performing their devotions at St Peter's Basilica or attending the weekly Wednesday Papal blessing, are likely also to visit the Sistine Chapel to admire its frescoes and to view the city's Roman ruins such as the Coliseum.

Pilgrimage, tourism, and indivisibility

As such it is difficult to clearly separate pilgrimage and tourism, especially when the same people stop their buses to pray earnestly at a shrine and then drop by at a scenic place or beach to take photographs or bathe. Such is the significance of sightseeing that tourism and cultural heritage have become a central marketing theme in many contemporary pilgrimage contexts, evident in the emphasis on cultural heritage in Shikoku and Santiago pilgrimage publicity, and boosted, in the case of Santiago, by its UNESCO World Heritage designation. The Camino has been promoted by Galician tourist authorities and in travel magazines as an ideal setting for walking holidays. The growing number of websites that advertise the services of travel agencies and tourist organizations that use phrases such as 'pilgrimage tourism' (a term found, for example, on the site of a major Indian tourist agency) also indicate how the two are increasingly contiguous. The intersections are emphasized when increasingly opulent facilities are being developed for the better-off who want to enjoy diverse attractions and visit religious sites in some comfort—as is happening in Mecca, with its new luxury hotels, and in places such as Shikoku and Hardwar.

While tourism and entertainment have played important roles in the development and popularity of pilgrimage historically, they are particularly powerful elements in its contemporary dynamics in a modern consumer-oriented world in which more people than ever before are able, due to modern transport and economic developments, to travel readily. Their wish to enjoy better facilities and combine pilgrimage and sightseeing, coupled with the readiness of those who benefit from or make their livings out of the pilgrimage trade to provide attractive facilities and diversions, has intensified the tourist aspects of pilgrimage. While this may be more evident in more highly developed economic contexts, it points to a general global pattern that appears to be emerging in modern pilgrimage.

Chapter 6
Secular sites and contemporary developments

If pilgrimage is found almost universally across religious traditions, it has also, in modern contexts, become widely associated with places that have no specific religious affiliations or links to formal religious traditions. Many of the themes associated with pilgrimage may be visible in a variety of settings that include visits to the graves and homes of deceased celebrities, war memorials, places associated with seminal political figures, and itineraries relating to the search for cultural roots, identity, and heritage. Moreover, those who participate in such visits may refer to their activities as pilgrimages and to themselves as pilgrims.

This is something that is especially, and perhaps increasingly, prevalent in the modern day, and particularly in Western contexts, where the term 'pilgrimage' is nowadays widely used by the mass media to describe such practices. Academics, too, have applied the term 'pilgrimage' to activities that occur outside of formal religious contexts but that incorporate modes of behaviour and phenomena similar to more traditional forms of pilgrimage. Frequently, too, the terms 'secular pilgrimage' and 'nonreligious pilgrimage' have become widely used in such contexts. Here we will look at some examples of activities that have been described as secular and nonreligious pilgrimages, along with other modern developments in which existing pilgrimage sites have acquired new dimensions and been reinterpreted in accord with contemporary trends, notably in the form of New Age activities.

At the right hand of the Lord

> Elvis, I know you sit at the right hand of the Lord.

This message is one of many that have been written on the wall outside Graceland, Elvis Presley's home in Memphis, USA (see Figure 13). When Presley died suddenly, aged 42, in 1977, people began to gather outside the house, many crying, praying, lighting candles, and leaving messages and offerings. People have been going to Graceland ever since, often acting similarly to those who converged there immediately after Elvis's death, and the offerings and messages they leave are sometimes tinged with religious allusions such as this one, associating Elvis and the Lord. Elvis's grave, in the Meditation Garden at Graceland, has an eternal flame dedicated by fans and is constantly adorned with offerings and messages, too, as crowds file by, many praying

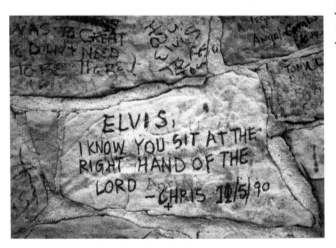

13. Inscription on the wall at Graceland.

14. Meditation Garden at Graceland: Elvis's Grave and Visitors.

as they seek to be close to him—something that they could never have managed while he was alive (see Figure 14). A statue of Christ stands near by.

During Elvis Memorial Week on the anniversary of his death, fans celebrate his life and music, and they also hold solemn vigils, light candles, pray, and even ask Elvis to intercede for them. Some talk about how they see Elvis as more than just a singer, but rather as a special figure to be venerated, and even, at times, credited with miraculous intercessions. Some come year after year and talk of their visits as an annual pilgrimage. Many also take away items such as stones and soil from Graceland's precincts, much in the way that pilgrims across time and cultures have taken home something of the places they have visited.

While not everyone who visits Graceland sees themselves as pilgrims—many are simply sightseers or fans keen to visit where he lived—pilgrimage remains a prominent motif at Graceland. The term is used, for example, by Elvis Presley Enterprises, which runs and markets Graceland, and whose website states that for Elvis fans 'Graceland is the ultimate pilgrimage'. Anyone who has been to pilgrimage sites such as Lourdes, Knock, Santiago, and Shikoku would also feel a sense of familiarity in Graceland's various souvenir shops that offer visitors plentiful opportunities for purchasing Elvis-related souvenirs.

Graceland is not unique in such terms, either as a place special to devotees of rock stars or as a site linked to graves and dramatic untimely deaths. The Parisian grave of Jim Morrison, lead singer of The Doors, who died aged 26, has repeatedly been covered with devotional messages and offerings by fans who come to honour his memory. In September 1973 one of the USA's greatest athletes, the long-distance runner Steve Prefontaine, was killed when his car crashed into a rock near Eugene, Oregon. The rock, known as Pre's Rock, has become a memorial to the athlete, visited by many, especially runners, who show their feelings for Prefontaine by leaving offerings, which range from running shirts and shoes to messages, candles, and prayers. Some have commented that they regard it as a place of contemplation, while messages and comments from visitors talk of how 'Pre' inspires them, sometimes incorporating quasi-religious themes that speak of him as an angel guiding them.

In all these contexts there is a recurrent theme of sadness and loss, generally associated with the premature demise of talented and charismatic figures who are believed to have had more to offer but who, in death, have become sources of inspiration and spiritual meaning. Their graves or death sites may then be memorialized and visited in ways similar to those of pilgrims to the tombs of saints.

War graves and the Vietnam Memorial

The sites of dreadful battles and mass loss of life, as well as war memorials commemorating the dead of such conflicts, are commonly visited by people paying homage to those who died and thinking about the meanings of their sacrifice. Often such visits, and the memorials themselves, express a vow or determination that such things should never again happen. The war graves of northern Europe, with their rows of simple white crosses and names of the fallen young men, for example, are testimony to the terrible carnage of World Wars One and Two, and have long been the focus of remembrance ceremonies and the expressed wish to prevent future wars.

After World War One, various organizations in the UK began arranging what they called pilgrimages to such war graves, to enable widows and mothers to see where their loved ones had died and been buried. The tradition continues to this day, with new generations continuing to visit the graves of deceased predecessors and keeping their memories alive. The travel branch of the British Legion, the charity that supports former soldiers and that organizes the UK's Remembrance services, arranges such remembrance tours and refers to them as pilgrimages on its website.

In Washington, DC, the Vietnam Memorial to the US military who fell in the Vietnam War has become a major site of remembrance, commemoration, and pilgrimage. The Wall, a simple, black marble slab sunk into the ground and inscribed chronologically with the names of all the US personnel who died in that war, provides a focal point for those who wish to honour the memory of fallen kin, friends, and comrades. Many visitors reflect silently before the Wall, seeking out particular names, praying, and leaving mementoes there—sometimes even making rubbings of names to take home with them.

For many visiting the Memorial is a pilgrimage. This is the term used by participants in the 'Run for the Wall', an annual cross-country motorbike ride of the Vietnam Veterans, from California to Washington, DC, which ends at the Wall, to honour fallen friends. Participants see their pilgrimage as a way of healing, on personal, individual, social, and national levels, the pain associated with the Vietnam War, which not only led to many thousands of deaths and bereaved families but caused huge divisions in the country. Veterans generally felt that they did not receive a proper welcome home after the war (for example, unlike troops returning from other conflicts, they had no homecoming parade) because of the internal national conflict it had caused. The pilgrimage helps them overcome this sense of grievance while healing their emotional wounds by enabling them to reconnect with American culture as they travel cross-country through the nation's stunning landscapes, staying in small towns, and receiving warm welcomes and hospitality from people along the way.

This goal of emotional healing is not just for those who fought in Vietnam but for all those who lost family members in the conflict, for those still classified as missing in action, and, in the eyes of participants, for the nation itself as it struggles to overcome the war's divisive scars. Riders stop at various memorials for Vietnam veterans along the route, and prayers are said each morning prior to setting out. The Wall is the physical end of the journey and its emotional climax, where the riders may pray, make rubbings, and leave offerings. In 1998, among the offerings left at the Wall were the ashes of a dead colleague, which riders had carried across country with them.

The Run is an emotional journey with many physical demands due to the long days spent on motorcycles. The bikes play an important emotional and symbolic role in the pilgrimage's structure and meanings; they are seen as representing intrinsic American values associated with individualism, the open road, and the freedom to travel. The idea of a communal brotherhood is also important, creating a feeling of the bikers being pilgrims together and emphasizing a sense of American emotional unity and togetherness. As such, the motorcycle pilgrimage across the American landscape to visit an American memorial and honour the fallen, encapsulates values and symbolic meanings linked to notions of American identity and national pride. As with many pilgrimages, some participants say they also feel a need to return year after year.

Political sites, leaders, and pilgrimage

Robben Island in South Africa, where Nelson Mandela was imprisoned for eighteen years, is now a museum and visitor site that has effectively become a place of pilgrimage for those seeking to learn about the struggle against Apartheid and to show their respect for Mandela. This was so even before Mandela's death in December 2013, with visits to the island an almost obligatory stop on the itineraries of foreign dignitaries. When the USA's President Obama and his family visited Robben Island in June 2013 (with Obama later giving a speech in which he stated how doing this had made him more aware of the sacrifices Mandela had made for the sake of freedom), the UK's *Guardian* newspaper described it as Obama's 'Mandela pilgrimage'. The term occurs frequently in the descriptions of those who visit the island, with Mandela's cell regarded as the most intense and moving part of each visitor's pilgrimage.

The island features also on a map produced, in March 2014, by South African Tourism, the official government tourist agency. Entitled 'Madiba's Journey', it encouraged travellers to follow in Nelson Mandela's footsteps through visiting sites in South Africa associated with his life story. While its intention was to encourage tourism in South Africa it was framed in the context of pilgrimage. Indeed, launching the project South Africa Tourism's chief executive stated that he wanted the world to view the journey through Mandela's footsteps as a pilgrimage and 'must-do' thing, in the same way that they might regard the pilgrimage to Mecca.

Mandela is but one of many political figures whose memorials or graves may be the focus of reverence and pilgrimage. Hundreds of thousands of Indonesians each year travel—sometimes on long journeys through the Indonesian archipelago—to visit the grave and mausoleum of Soekarno (1901–70), leader of Indonesia's independence struggle and its first president. While some come to honour a political leader, many demonstrate religious levels of devotion to him, burning incense at the grave and praying to him for help in their personal lives. Many, viewing him as a unifying national figure, also invoke his help in solving the nation's problems.

Lenin's tomb and mausoleum in Moscow is another example, one that points to a recurrent theme among Communist regimes whose ideological stance led them to try to eradicate organized religion. To this end such regimes created secularized state cults based around state rituals and heroes who were elevated as figures of public reverence. When Lenin died in 1924, he became a major focus of this state secular cult in the Soviet Union. Proclaimed as a prophet of the revolution, his body was embalmed and placed in a mausoleum in Red Square, which became a de facto pilgrimage shrine. Throughout the Communist era millions of people travelled to Moscow to file past his body and pay their respects; for state officials and party members it was an especially important ritual. While the collapse of Communism, the demise of the Soviet Union, and the removal of earlier restrictions on organized religions have undermined this state-centred cult, Lenin's mausoleum continues to attract some who bow reverently, although nowadays it is more clearly, for most visitors, simply an attraction on the Moscow tourist trail.

Similarly Mao-Tse Tung's mausoleum in Beijing, containing his embalmed body, was designed to preserve his memory, immortalize him and his teachings, and inspire others to follow his path. During Mao's lifetime, especially during the Cultural Revolution of the mid-1960s, his regime emphasized places along the path of his revolutionary struggle as sites of pilgrimage to be visited by young cadres. At his death the regime built a mausoleum incorporating a variety of cultural and quasi-religious images from China's history to further underline this motif. The granite slab of his tomb, for example, came from Tai Shan, one of China's historic sacred mountains. Visits to the mausoleum, especially in the early years after his death, were solemn; for Communist Party officials it was a necessary site of pilgrimage. Again, as with Lenin's mausoleum, as the regime has changed and with it Mao's memory, it has become predominantly a place on Beijing's tourist itinerary, although observers note that some, particularly older, Chinese visitors may still make offerings there.

Accounts of the mausoleum of Kim Il-Sung, the first Communist dictator of North Korea, and of his son and successor Kim Jong-il, indicate that this is a major pilgrimage site for a state that represses religion but that has fostered an extraordinary cult of devotion to its leaders. Visitors must wear formal clothing to enter. They file past murals depicting scenes of mourning at the leaders' demise and exhibitions of their lives, and pass through purification devices to remove dust from their clothes prior to 'meeting' the embalmed ex-leaders and, finally, to the accompaniment of solemn music, they bow and perform acts of reverence before the tombs.

Roots, identity, pilgrimage

Journeying to places associated with one's ancestral roots is frequently seen as a modern form of pilgrimage associated with issues of quest, personal search, and identity. Such 'roots pilgrimages' are particularly poignant and important for those who are aware that their ancestors were immigrants and that their hereditary roots are initially from another country, as is common in North America, for example. Many Americans of European ancestry, for instance, travel back to the lands from which their forefathers emigrated. Such journeys to places of family origin are also associated with that recurrent question commonly asked by pilgrims: 'who am I?'

Roots pilgrimages and the search for identity and meaning have become especially significant for African Americans, who travel to the continent from whence their ancestors were forcefully brought as slaves, and for whom Africa is seen as a spiritual homeland. A major factor in this context was the work of African American author Alex Haley, whose *Roots: The Saga of an American Family* was published in 1976 and then became a widely watched television series. In *Roots* Haley traced, in fictionalized form, his familial ancestral roots back to The Gambia in West Africa. Exploring issues of identity and belonging set in the context of suffering and slavery, it generated massive interest among African Americans and led many to affirm their African heritage, visit places associated with it, and pay homage to the grief and suffering of their ancestors. Subsequently, a growing number of tours and events have developed to facilitate such pursuits. Each year The Gambia hosts an annual Roots Homecoming Festival, while sites where slaves were held prior to being shipped to the Americas, such as the castles on the Ghanaian coast and Gorée, the island off Dakar in Senegal, have become important places on such roots pilgrimage itineraries.

Those going to Africa to seek their roots at times talk about their journeys as pilgrimages and as a return to their spiritual homeland. Companies and organizations, with names such as African Pilgrimages Incorporated, arrange and facilitate similar visits, portraying them as a form of remembrance and reconciliation among people of African heritage. These roots pilgrimages contain themes recurrent in pilgrimage contexts: a return to one's origins; concepts of a spiritually charged and special sacred place; a search for a sense of identity; remembrance through retracing the footsteps of significant figures of the past (in this context, one's ancestors); and bids to encounter and seek to heal the emotional pains of the past.

Fan culture and pilgrimage

Fan culture is another area where the image of pilgrimage has been widely adopted. The industry that has developed around sites associated with The Beatles in England, for example, uses the term in association with tours for Beatles fans from around the world, who visit places associated with the group in their hometown Liverpool; and in London, where the Abbey Road street crossing is a highlight. On personal websites and blogs, too, some fans speak of their visits to such special places as being their personal Beatles pilgrimages.

Pilgrimage motifs have been widely adopted also in Japan to refer to places associated with popular entertainment and fan culture. There is widespread interest displayed by (for the most part, younger male) fans to visit real locations that have appeared in well-known anime films or manga cartoons. The result has been the development of what are referred to (and advertised as) *manga junrei* ('manga pilgrimages') and *anime junrei*, both of which involve visiting a number of famed sites. *Junrei* as was earlier noted, is commonly used in Japanese to refer to pilgrimages that incorporate a number of linked sites. The term *seichi* ('sacred place') is sometimes also used in this context: there are manga and anime *seichi junrei* routes. These pilgrimages are so popular that there is even a telephone application (the *Seichi Junrei* App), which can be downloaded and used to find out more about the sites on the routes and then to share information about them with other fans. Municipalities and regional tourist agencies whose locations feature in popular manga or anime productions have been proactive in using such motifs to create and promote such pilgrimage routes, meaning that some of the religious sites on these routes have seen their visitor numbers grow exponentially. For instance, after an anime film featured in its opening shots the relatively unknown Washinomiya Shrine in Saitama, near Tokyo, visitor numbers shot up. The numbers of visitors attending its annual *hatsumōde* (New Year visiting ritual, which is itself a form of pilgrimage), soared, increasing fivefold—from 90,000 to 450,000 between 2007 and 2010.

Hiking trails as pilgrimages

The successful depiction of the Santiago pilgrimage as a European cultural itinerary has been a catalyst for the development or invention of other routes by various national and regional development and tourist agencies intent on capitalizing on contemporary interests in hiking and pilgrimage. In Norway, for example, Nidaros Cathedral in Trondheim houses the tomb of King Olaf Haraldsson, who died in 1030 and was later canonized as St Olaf. Based on the claim that an ancient pilgrimage way used to lead across Norway to the cathedral, St Olav's Way was inaugurated in 1997 and heavily promoted by Norway's official tourism agency as a hiking trail through which one could encounter the country's cultural and religious heritage while enjoying splendid scenery. Emphasizing hiking and landscape, it has been proclaimed as a European cultural route under the auspices of the Council of Europe (which had previously given similar accreditation to the Santiago Camino).

The Ireland and Northern Ireland Tourist Boards, in 2009, jointly commissioned a feasibility study about the construction of a similar trail in Ireland—St Patrick's Way. Based on the observation that hiking along pilgrimage trails has become an increasingly popular activity and drawing on information from various pilgrimages around the world, including those of Santiago and Shikoku, to garner information on how to develop and promote such itineraries, the project, still in the developmental stage, is seeking to create a St Patrick-based pilgrimage and cultural itinerary that will appeal to hikers and tourists.

Pilgrimage and the 'New Age'

If secular or nonreligious pilgrimages are one area of contemporary interest and growth, another focuses on the ways in which pilgrimage practices and places may be revitalized or appropriated by new trends. Pilgrimage has been used and adopted as a means of personal spiritual search by advocates of the 'New Age'—a somewhat loose term that indicates an eclectic amalgam of notions including the rejection of religion as a traditional, organized entity while incorporating all manner of quasi-religious ideas and imaginings that are attributed to various spiritual traditions. New Age ideas are centred on individualized concepts of spiritual development, and notions of holistic healing and the integrated nature of the mind, body, and spirit.

Authors such as Phil Cousineau, whose *The Art of Pilgrimage* presents pilgrimage as a 'spirit-renewing ritual' and offers advice on how to transform ordinary journeys into sacred ones, have put a New Age spin on pilgrimage. Paulo Coelho and Shirley MacLaine have done the same, with their articulation of pilgrimages to Santiago seen through a lens of contemporary spiritual self-discovery. The pilgrims who in the present day walk to Santiago or around Shikoku and express ideas of personal search, while stating that they have no religious affiliation, are examples of this trend.

New Age themes have also permeated some traditional pilgrimage sites and given them new orientations in modern times. Sedona in Arizona, a desert location with pre-existing significance in Native American cultural contexts, has emerged in recent times as a centre for New Age activities. Its dramatic landscape, regularly used as a setting for Hollywood movies and television advertisements, was instrumental in attracting the attention of New Age seekers who viewed it as a repository of sacred power expressing in physical form the contours of a spiritual realm. Local business interests such as the Sedona Tourism Bureau and Chamber of Commerce, whose website refers to Sedona as 'a spiritual mecca and global power spot', played their part in promoting it as an especially significant place where seekers could access new spiritual truths.

Advocates claim it to be a 'power spot' (a place of concentrated spiritual energy) where various 'vortexes'—a term coined by a local medium to indicate special concentrations of energy within the wider 'power spot'—can be accessed. Moreover, stories of dramatic phenomena and miraculous happenings around these so-called vortexes have been spread among those journeying to Sedona. Various books and other publications proclaiming the power of Sedona's 'vortexes' and offering advice on how people can experience and use them as sites for meditation and rituals have further heightened the image of a place suffused with spiritual power. All this has helped to make Sedona into a New Age pilgrimage centre, as have the commercial developments and infrastructures that have sprung up to cater for the needs and interests of the new waves of pilgrims. These include shops selling New Age goods, people claiming to be spiritual teachers and healers, and organized 'vortex tours'.

Glastonbury, in Somerset, England, has also been adopted as New Age pilgrimage centre. It has a long history as a pilgrimage site. Legends associate it with Joseph of Arimathea and the Holy Grail, and its Abbey has attracted pilgrims since the 13th century. It is also claimed—with scant or nonexistent historical support—as the site of Avalon in England's legends of King Arthur and as an ancient spiritual centre for various traditions, including the druid and goddess cults, which according to their modern proponents operated in England prior to being submerged by the development of Christianity. Glastonbury's fascinating geography—formerly being an island set in a low-lying area dominated by the Tor, a steep hill on the town's outskirts—has, as with Sedona, been central to its appeal, leading numerous seekers and enthusiasts over the ages to imagine and find spiritual meaning in its landscape.

Since the early 20th century, enthusiasts of alternative therapies and people claiming associations with a variety of spiritual traditions including goddess cults, paganism, and New Age healing, have been going to Glastonbury. In so doing, they frequently describe themselves as pilgrims as they seek mystical

and transformative experiences in a landscape that they claim
is bathed in special spiritual forces. Some also see their presence
in Glastonbury as a means of reclaiming or returning to a
lost spiritual heritage that they claim existed there prior to
Christianity. As at Sedona many have stayed to make a living by
providing services for other visitors and thereby further enhancing
Glastonbury's cultic status. Various healing centres, new places of
worship (including a goddess temple), and individuals offering
various spiritual services are found throughout the town. There
are shops there providing goods associated with aspects of New
Age culture such as pendants, crystals, and aromatherapy
materials. Both the Tor and areas around the town are the focus of
a variety of meditative, ritual, and ceremonial activities by various
groups and individuals alike.

There are still Christian pilgrimages organized to Glastonbury
in both the Anglican and Catholic traditions, with each holding
an annual pilgrimage to the site—for the Anglicans it is every
June, with church services and a street procession; and for the
Catholics it is in July. However, the 'alternative' and diverse
New Age traditions are the most dominant manifestations of
pilgrimage activity nowadays at Glastonbury. In both Sedona and
Glastonbury existing places of pilgrimage and religious practice
have been ascribed new meanings by new waves of pilgrims
who, in proclaiming them as specially charged landscapes and
gateways to spiritual realms, have added new layers to these
sites and reinvented them in ways attractive to new generations
of seekers.

Labyrinths

Another example of modern pilgrimage reinterpretation and
reinvention relates to labyrinths. Labyrinths have one pathway,
which leads from their entrance to the centre, usually winding
through all its segments to get there. These labyrinths can be
found on the floors of various medieval European churches and

cathedrals, perhaps the most famous of which is at Chartres
Cathedral in France, whose labyrinth dates from the 13th century
and has four sectors, eleven concentric winding pathways, and
twenty-eight loops leading to its centre. Although various forms
of labyrinth have been found across cultures back into antiquity,
they particularly appeared in churches around the time that the
physical journey to Jerusalem and the Christian Holy Land
become problematic after the Crusades, for one of their roles was
as a substitute for the pilgrimage to the Holy Land.

These labyrinths, known as 'Jerusalems' or 'chemin de Jérusalem'
(road to Jerusalem), served as a means by which pilgrims could,
symbolically and in microcosm, perform the distant and difficult
journey to Jerusalem by walking meditatively to their centres.
Walking through a labyrinth was also seen as a form of spiritual
contemplation and metaphorical journey through the vagaries
of life; the Chartres labyrinth was also known as the 'chemin de
paradis': the road to paradise. Walking through its twists and
turns served as a metaphor for the pilgrimage of life, from birth to
death, as one progressed to the centre, and then, as one exited, to
resurrection and entry into heaven.

Practices associated with labyrinths fell into abeyance by the
18th century (suppressed, according to some, by the Catholic
Church), but since the 1990s interest in them has been revived by
various societies and practitioners advocating the labyrinth as a
form of meditative spiritual practice and symbolic pilgrimage
towards self-realization. A significant figure here has been Lauren
Artress, a canon at Grace Cathedral, San Francisco, who visited
Chartres with colleagues, walked its labyrinth, and introduced
the concept to Grace Cathedral, which now has two labyrinths
modelled on Chartres (see Figure 15). She published a book in
1995 focusing on the labyrinth as a spiritual tool; founded an
organization promoting labyrinths as a means of transforming
the human spirit; and now conducts workshops and lectures
widely on the topic.

15. Overhead view of one of the labyrinths inside Grace Cathedral, San Francisco.

Others, too, have focused on the labyrinth as a mode of spiritual pilgrimage, prayer, and meditation. Unsurprisingly a veritable industry of books and online guides on how to use labyrinths as a map for personal awareness and self-help, as a means of finding inner sanctity, and even on how to build one's own labyrinth, has developed. International societies such as Veriditas (Artress's organization) and The Labyrinth Society, both formed in the 1990s, also promote the concept. Neither has any formal religious affiliations but they both talk about labyrinths as pathways for spiritual discovery and individualized awareness in terms not dissimilar to those used by New Agers. The result has been that many new labyrinths have appeared in recent years including at least two at British universities: at Edinburgh University and at the University of Kent.

Labyrinths have thus been revitalized as a form of pilgrimage in miniature in which individuals tread a path of self-awareness and realization. They reflect another dimension of contemporary development and reinterpretation and, as with the profusion of New Age themes now evident at places such as Glastonbury and Sedona, indicate how traditional practices and places can be infused with new meanings as a pilgrimage-oriented practice based in a particular religious tradition is reinterpreted in line with contemporary notions of spirituality.

The evolving world of pilgrimage

The previous examples indicate that pilgrimage need not be just about formal religious traditions. Pilgrimage themes identified in Chapter 2—of landscapes and places imbued with deep meanings and as sources of special powers and graces for those who visit or walk through them, of associations with special and emotionally significant figures, and of travel to and through such places—are also present in secular contexts and at places with no formal religious connections. So are practices commonly associated with pilgrimage to religious sites, such as memorializing and paying reverence to a special figure, communing with the dead, making physical journeys that are spiritually symbolic, seeking emotional healing and searching for inspiration and personal meaning.

The ways in which existing sites may be reinterpreted or adapted within the contours of new religious phenomena, as, for example, at Glastonbury, and in which earlier traditions of pilgrimage re-enactment may be revived and reinterpreted, as with labyrinths, indicate how pilgrimages can shift across religious boundaries and be reinvented and recalibrated. They are further indications of how pilgrimage is continually reshaped to fit with the contours of the age and of the seemingly recurrent human wish for and interest in finding or creating new ways and places through which to engage in such practices.

The modern era has brought undoubtedly the most striking developments in the world of pilgrimage. These range from the rise of mass transportation systems aligned to modern economies that have expanded the potential number of people who can afford the time and costs of travel, to an increasing convergence of tourist and religious themes, to an increasing focus on issues of heritage and cultural identity, and to the emergence of new places to incorporate within the wider pilgrimage spectrum. The growth of tourism as a global industry has not marginalized pilgrimage so much as given it added stimulus—as have contemporary interests in history, identity, roots, and heritage.

Modern developments have certainly made pilgrimage a safer, generally more comfortable, option than in earlier eras when dangers and death were a constant menace. They have democratized pilgrimage by enabling more people, from more strata of society and from wider age groups, to do it than in in any previous age. That certainly provides a strong counter-argument to any criticisms that modern developments and commercial growth have diminished the ascetic and religious orientations of pilgrimage, and to worries sometimes expressed by religious authorities that modern growth might increase playful tourist activities around their sites and so minimize their solemn faith-based aspects. However, recent developments have not, in fact, excluded the potential for asceticism or faith, as the pilgrims who choose to walk the Amarnath, Santiago, and Shikoku pilgrimages, or to go on their hands and knees at places such as at Tinos, indicate.

Influenced by changing contexts, conditions, and technologies, pilgrimage, as befits a practice associated with transience and movement, is never static in nature. Yet it is also underpinned by many continuities. A 14th or 15th century pilgrim transported miraculously to contemporary Shikoku or the Santiago Camino would no doubt feel bemused at the buses full of older women who speed round Shikoku in ten or so days; and the youthful backpackers, with their hiking gear and seemingly little interest in the narratives of St James and the quest for Christian salvation, who hike the Camino. Muslims having made an arduous journey over many months to Mecca some centuries back might be astonished at the scenes nowadays of millions flying in to enjoy its modern facilities and hotels. However, in both these cases, they would doubtless recognize similarities too. In the *hajj* the same rituals are performed. Modern pilgrims may also be praying to and invoking holy figures, and hoping for salvation and benefits for themselves and their dead kin. They are still expressing that sense of restlessness, transience, and searching for meaning that has run through pilgrim attitudes over the centuries.

Historical consciousness and common identities, too, permeate their pilgrimages. Muslims, as they run through air-conditioned tunnels during the *hajj*, are still re-enacting an ancient ritual that speaks to the heart of their tradition, done by generations of pilgrims before them, and that connects present, past, and future pilgrims in a continuing global community of shared faith. Pilgrims elsewhere are also engaged in activities carried out by past generations and may well sense this continuity in their actions. Those on routes such as Santiago and Shikoku may be aware of previous eras of pilgrims who walked that same path while Hindus carrying the ashes of their ancestors to a sacred river crossing in India may be conscious that their forefathers did this too.

What is certainly recurrent and seemingly unchanging is the desire of people to get away, even if temporarily, from their everyday circumstances, to look for new meanings and reaffirmations of personal identities, and to go to places that they feel can help them in such quests. So, too, are their hopes that this will enrich their lives, offering them spiritual and other benefits, and enabling them to encounter and commune with figures and powers that they believe reside and can be accessed in the places they go to. Pilgrimage offers such opportunities, which is why so many places have developed and been sought out by pilgrims and promoted by religious and other authorities over the ages. It is why new places of pilgrimage are continually being created, and why communities that move across cultures and environments, as with Hindu migrants to the UK and USA, or Japanese to Hawaii, feel the need to recreate their traditional pilgrimage sites in their new homelands.

As such, pilgrimage has been a recurrent theme in religious contexts, and nowadays increasingly in more clearly nonreligious ones, that offers scope for self-development, escape, faith, and hope, as well as play and entertainment. It will doubtless remain attractive to people in coming generations, too, although one should not be surprised if they added new interpretations and modes of travel (and things to bring home with them), and developed new places to visit, alongside reaffirming the value of older sites and routes. Continually adapting to the circumstances, needs, and wishes of its time, pilgrimage remains one of the most significant reasons why people have travelled historically and in the present, and one of the core elements in the religious world and beyond.

Further reading

While I have listed readings under each chapter, several of the items listed below are useful for a variety of chapters.

Chapter 1: Pilgrimage around the world

Coleman, Simon and John Elsner. 1995. *Pilgrimage Past and Present in the World Religions*. Cambridge, MA: Harvard University Press.

Gold, Ann Grodzins. 1989. *Fruitful Journeys: The Ways of Rajasthani Pilgrims*. Berkeley and Los Angeles: University of California Press.

Lochtefeld, James G. 2010. *God's Gateway: Identity and Meaning in a Hindu Pilgrimage Place*. Oxford and New York: Oxford University Press.

Reader, Ian. 2005. *Making Pilgrimages: Meaning and Practice in Shikoku*. Honolulu: University of Hawaii Press.

Rudolph, Conrad. 2004. *Pilgrimage to the End of the World: The Road to Santiago de Compostela*. Chicago: University of Chicago Press.

Turner, Victor and Edith. 1978. *Image and Pilgrimage in Christian Culture*. Oxford: Blackwell.

Chapter 2: Forms, themes, and meanings

Brown, Peter. 2009. *The Cult of Saints: Its Rise and Function in Latin Christianity*. Chicago: University Chicago Press.

Dubisch, Jill. 1995. *In a Different Place: Pilgrimage, Gender, and Practice at a Greek Island Shrine*. Princeton, NJ: Princeton University Press.

Eade, John and Michael Sallnow (eds). 1991. *Contesting the Sacred: The Anthropology of Christian Pilgrimage*. London: Routledge.

Feldhaus, Anne. 2004. *Connected Places: Region, Pilgrimage, and Geographical Imagination in India*. New York and Basingstoke: Palgrave Macmillan.

Geary, Patrick J. 1991. *Furta Sacra: Thefts of Relics in the Central Middle Ages*. Princeton, NJ: Princeton University Press.

Harris, Ruth. 1999. *Lourdes: Body and Spirit in the Secular Age*. Harmondsworth: Penguin.

Huber, Toni. 2008. *The Holy Land Reborn: Pilgrimage and the Reinvention of Buddhist India*. Chicago: University of Chicago Press.

Naquin, Susan and Chün-Fang Yü (eds). 1992. *Pilgrims and Sacred Sites in China*. Berkeley, Los Angeles, and Oxford: University of California Press.

Reader, Ian and Paul L. Swanson. 1997. Editors' Introduction: Pilgrimage in the Japanese Religious Tradition. *Japanese Journal of Religious Studies* Vol. 24, Nos. 3–4, pp. 225–70.

Chapter 3: More than miracles

Bianchi, Robert R. 2004. *Guests of God—Pilgrimage and Politics in the Islamic World*. New York: Oxford University Press.

Foster, Georgana and Robert Stoddard. 2010. Vaishno Devi, the Most Famous Goddess Shrine in the Siwālik. In Rana P. B. Singh (ed.) *Sacred Geography of Goddesses in South Asia*. Newcastle upon Tyne: Cambridge Scholars Press, pp. 109–24.

Kaufman, Suzanne K. 2004. *Consuming Visions: Mass Culture and the Lourdes Shrine*. Ithaca, NY: Cornell University Press.

Peters, F. E. 1995. *The Hajj: The Muslim Pilgrimage to Mecca and the Holy Places*. Princeton, NJ: Princeton University Press.

Reader, Ian. 2014. *Pilgrimage in the Marketplace*. New York and Abingdon: Routledge.

Taylor, Philip. 2004. *Goddess on the Rise: Pilgrimage and Popular Religion in Vietnam*. Honolulu: University of Hawaii Press.

Chapter 4: Practices, motives, and experiences

Chareyron, Nicole. 2000. *Pilgrims to Jerusalem in the Middle Ages*. New York: Columbia University Press.

Coleman, Simon. 2000. Meanings of Movement, Place and Home at Walsingham. *Culture and Religion* Vol. 1, No. 2, pp. 153–70.

Frey, Nancy Louise. 1998. *Pilgrim Stories: On and Off the Road to Santiago.* Berkeley, CA, University of California Press.

Fuller, Christopher. 1992. *The Camphor Flame: Popular Hinduism and Society in India.* Princeton, NJ: Princeton University Press, Chapter 9, pp. 204–23.

Hammoudi, Abdellah. 2006. *A Season in Mecca: Narrative of a Pilgrimage.* Cambridge: Polity.

Sumption, Jonathan. 1975. *Pilgrimage: An Image of Mediaeval Religion.* London: Faber and Faber.

Webb, Diana. 2000. *Pilgrimage in Medieval England.* London: Hambledon and London.

Chapter 5: Festivity, tourism, and souvenirs

Badone, Ellen and Sharon R. Roseman (eds). 2004. *Intersecting Journeys: The Anthropology of Pilgrimage and Tourism.* Urbana and Chicago: University of Illinois Press.

Gladstone, David L. 2005. *From Pilgrimage to Package Tour: Travel and Tourism in the Third World.* London: Routledge.

Norman, Alex. 2011. *Spiritual Tourism: Travel and Religious Practice in Western Society.* London: Bloomsbury.

Stausberg, Michael. 2010. *Religion and Tourism: Crossroads, Destinations and Encounters.* London and New York: Routledge.

Thal, Sarah. 2005. *Rearranging the Landscape of the Gods: The Politics of a Pilgrimage Site in Japan, 1573–1912.* Chicago: University of Chicago Press.

Timothy, Dallen J. and Daniel H. Olsen (eds). 2006. *Tourism, Religion and Spiritual Journeys.* London: Routledge.

(see also Reader 2014 listed under Chapter 3.)

Chapter 6: Secular sites and contemporary developments

Beaman, Lori. 2006. Labyrinth as Heterotopia: The Pilgrim's Creation of Space. In Swatos, William Jr (ed.) *On the Road to Being There: Continuing the Pilgrimage-Tourism Dialogue.* Leiden: Brill Academic Press, pp. 83–103.

Ivakhiv, Adrian J. 2001. *Claiming Sacred Ground: Pilgrims and Politics at Glastonbury and Sedona*. Bloomington: Indiana University Press.

Margry, Peter Jan (ed.) 2008. *Shrines and Pilgrimage in the Modern World: New Itineraries into the Sacred*. Amsterdam: Amsterdam University Press.

Michalowski, Raymond and Jill Dubisch. 2001. *Run for the Wall: Remembering Vietnam on a Motorcycle Pilgrimage*. New Brunswick, NJ: Rutgers University Press.

Reader, Ian and Tony Walter (eds). 1993. *Pilgrimage in Popular Culture*. Basingstoke and New York: Palgrave.

Pilgrimage

Index

Pilgrimage